W9-CIO-007

The Modern Language Association of America

Approaches to Teaching
Masterpieces of World Literature

Joseph Gibaldi, Series Editor

Approaches to Teaching Melville's *Moby-Dick*

Edited by

Martin Bickman

The Modern Language Association of America
New York   1985

Library of Congress Cataloging in Publication Data
Main entry under title:

Approaches to teaching Melville's Moby-Dick.

(Approaches to teaching masterpieces of
world literature; 8)
    Bibliography: p.
    Includes index.
    1. Melville, Herman, 1819–1891. Moby Dick—
Addresses, essays, lectures. 2. Melville, Herman,
1819–1891—Study and teaching—Addresses, essays,
lectures. I. Bickman, Martin, 1945–   . II. Series.
PS2384.M62A66 1985   813'.3   85-4892
ISBN 0-87352-489-6
ISBN 0-87352-490-X (pbk.)

The MLA wishes to thank Edouard Stackpole, curator of the Peter Foulger Museum,
Nantucket, Massachusetts, for the cover illustration in the paperback edition.

Published by The Modern Language Association of America
Astor Place, New York, New York

CONTENTS

PREFACE TO THE SERIES

In *The Art of Teaching* Gilbert Highet wrote, "Bad teaching wastes a great deal of effort, and spoils many lives which might have been full of energy and happiness." All too many teachers have failed in their work, Highet argued, simply "because they have not thought about it." We hope that the Approaches to Teaching Masterpieces of World Literature series, sponsored by the Modern Language Association's Committee on Teaching and Related Professional Activities, will not only improve the craft—as well as the art—of teaching but also encourage serious and continuing discussion of the aims and methods of teaching literature.

The principal objective of the series is to collect within each volume a number of points of view on teaching a specific work of world literature, a literary tradition, or a writer widely taught at the undergraduate level. Preparation begins with a wide-ranging survey of instructors, which enables us to include in the volume the philosophies and approaches, thoughts and methods of scores of experienced teachers. The result is a sourcebook of material, information, and ideas on teaching the subject to undergraduates.

The series is intended to serve nonspecialists as well as specialists, inexperienced as well as experienced teachers, graduate students who wish to learn effective ways of teaching as well as senior professors who wish to compare their own approaches with the approaches of colleagues in other schools. Of course, no volume in the series can ever substitute for erudition, intelligence, creativity, and sensitivity in teaching. We hope merely that each book will point readers in useful directions; at most each will offer only a first step in the long journey to successful teaching. We may perhaps adopt as keynote for the series Alfred North Whitehead's observation in *The Aims of Education* that a liberal education "proceeds by imparting a knowledge of the masterpieces of thought, of imaginative literature, and of art."

Joseph Gibaldi
Series Editor

PREFACE TO THE VOLUME

Herman Melville, once a country schoolmaster himself, has *Moby-Dick*'s narrator, another former schoolmaster, say of the physical and metaphysical implications of the whale's circulatory system, "But how easy and how hopeless to teach these fine things!" (Hayford and Parker 261; ch. 68; all quotations from *Moby-Dick* are taken from this edition). Ishmael's exclamation is reflected in the two purposes of this volume, purposes that are sometimes at odds with each other. The first is to provide direct practical aid, particularly to teachers who are less familiar than they would like with the novel and its contexts. Here is a starter kit, distilled in large part from the responses to a lengthy and intrusive questionnaire of 139 teachers and 72 students who studied *Moby-Dick* with these teachers. From these questionnaires a range of consensus emerges on basic issues such as texts, secondary readings, resources. The publication of this volume means that every teacher need not begin again alone to reinvent *The Whale*.

The other purpose of this volume, though, is to stimulate the teacher's own resourcefulness and creativity, to help him or her become a more self-aware and sensitive instructor. The writers of the essays in the Approaches section were chosen from the larger pool of respondents not only because they had particularly helpful comments on teaching the book but also because they challenge our own unexamined assumptions and calcified procedures. It may indeed be hopeless to try to teach somebody how to read or think or teach, but one can open possibilities and set forth positions against which other teachers must define themselves; one can stake out an interpretation or create a structure for teaching, which others can adapt, modify, or completely reverse.

Indeed, this process of endless revision and reformulation is particularly relevant to *Moby-Dick* and is one of the factors that make it such a frustrating yet powerful book to teach. *Moby-Dick* constantly invites us to construct interpretations, to search for coherences, to ferret out symbolic resonances, to find structural patterns. At the same time, it seems to undercut these attempts, to reverse expectations, to give urgent voice to the opposing visions. I do not argue that the ultimate stance of the book is antinomian, nihilistic, or absurdist. Rather, Melville is suspicious of any finalities abstracted from the processes through which they were attained. Ishmael tells us that the only way to know the whale is as it exists, at flux in its element of flux, and not in any static rendering. Further, as Ishmael tells it, "any human thing supposed to be complete, must for that very reason infallibly be faulty. . . . God keep me from ever completing anything" (118, 128; ch. 32).

The urgent analogy for us is that to know this book—perhaps any book, but certainly this one—we must engage in a constant process of interpretation, qualification, revision, and reinterpretation. If we as teachers have our own line on the book, that line is useful only as a hypothesis to test in the interplay of a class and in scrutiny against specific passages, not as something to be inscribed directly in student notebooks without passing through their own critical sensibilities. Similarly, our task is not simply to have our students produce interpretations of the book. The difficulties many of them face in reading and writing relate not so much to their inability to make meanings as to their tendency to make meanings too quickly, to leap to easy, even glib, conclusions. To deepen and enrich the act of interpretation we have to go beyond the silent activities of reading and thinking and to involve students in speaking and writing about the book, articulating responses to which we and their classmates then respond, so they can be further refined, clarified, made more inclusive, more supple and subtle. Melville's own example and explicit statements warn us against giving our students only a "final" exam or paper on the book.

I set these points out here not because they are necessarily shared by all the other contributors or are the most important things to say about teaching the book, but because this volume will be most useful if each statement in it is taken as provisional and open, if everything here is viewed as "but a draught—nay, but the draught of a draught" (128; ch. 32). (And we see Ishmael revising his words in the very act of writing them.) The various viewpoints and voices have to be seen dialectically—both with one another and with each teacher's experience of reading and working with the book.

Of my many debts and gratitudes, the primary ones are to the instructors and students who responded so generously to the questionnaires at an especially harried time, the end of the academic year. Indeed, the single most gratifying finding from the questionnaires is the evidence that so much thought and care is put into day-to-day teaching. While we should not elevate this impression into a scientific discovery—the instructors who did respond were a self-selecting group—still, the number of these teachers, their distribution throughout all strata of the MLA membership, the hard, detailed work that went into so many syllabi, study questions, guides, and outlines suggest how much of our work is revealed only in the relative privacies of our own classrooms. This volume is a modest effort to invade that unofficial silence, to let us share those parts of our professional lives that are perhaps the most worth sharing.

The debt mentioned above is multiplied in the case of those respondents who agreed to elaborate on their questionnaire answers in the form of the articles that make up the Approaches section. This volume has been a collaboration in the sense not only of a work done by many hands but of an active and often heady and heated exchange of ideas. Contributors read one another's articles and provided constructive suggestions and incisive critiques. Aside from those teachers listed on the contents page, I mention in particular several lynx-eyed readers and advisors: Joyce Sparer Adler, Howard Horsford, Bruce Kawin, Lee Krauth, Claude Richard, and Merton Sealts. Cynthia Conroy and later Janet Somerville provided valuable research and editorial assistance, along with constant good humor and enthusiasm. Ms. Somerville, who shared with me her own unpublished work on *Moby-Dick*, often saved me and other contributors from sins of omission and commission. Marje Urban was patient and accurate in typing a much rearranged manuscript. Joseph Gibaldi at the MLA initiated this project and was a constant source of good judgment and support. As always, I owe the most to my wife, Louise, who in spite of—or perhaps because of—her own busy career was a perennial source of perspective, encouragement, concern, and delight.

MB

Part One

MATERIALS

Martin Bickman

Extracts

In compiling this Materials section I chewed up, digested, and—for the sake of brevity—homogenized the suggestions of many respondents to the instructor and student questionnaires. It would be a mistake, though, not to give the reader a sense of the variety of perspectives, the multiplicity of voices, the richness of texture in the questionnaires, and these somewhat random, higgledy-piggledy extracts are small steps in that direction.

I talk most of the time. I know more than the students do. Else why would I be teaching them?

I talk a great deal of the time. Their questions tend to bring me back to reality with a jerk.

The ideal class would consist of my asking the perfect question and not saying another word. Students, like water, find their own level—and it's a surprisingly high one. My hope is that the question could not really be summed up in an answer by the end of any discussion, but could, like all good criticism of life, go on constantly renewed and endless in its possibilities. That is really all the detail that is necessary. I often fail to find the best question, and then I have to resort to footnoting and lecturing and slinging the usual "expertise," always a sign of failure. . . . I think the great thing about *MD* is that no conclusion about it can be more than tentative and ambiguous, which is to a great extent, of course, what the book is about.

Students have trouble persevering, but my approach insists upon the symbolic importance of the cetological details. I have to work hard at selling this view, but it comprises what is always for me a very enjoyable teaching experience.

I have come to think of Herman Melville as a nautical writer first, a symbolic giant second. This is refreshing and makes sense of more of the book (at least quantitatively). The risks of literalism are less than those of arcane symbolism.

I try to focus on various characters' views of the whale. Then I jump on Starbuck & claim (with deliberate excess) that he's a gutless turkey. Then the students defend him & I retreat (moderately). I isolate Starbuck since he seems in many ways to typify the "modern predicament."

3

I tend to "try out" in discussion new and sometimes (from my point of view) wacky interpretations. Examining the lunatic fringe can sometimes make members of the class more confident of their own perceptions.

I have abandoned the "sacred text" approach to literature. I cannot, therefore, see any real purpose to this project.

Last year my encounter with *Moby-Dick* was deep; it was disturbing, terrifying, and joyful. . . . it was my own struggle with the ungraspable phantom of life. At the risk of being eternally stove and sunk, I fully and deeply explored the Ishmael and the Ahab within myself and I survived.

I linger over words, puns, language, the movement from dream to articulated speech.

It is a novel of process and the reader is necessary to its shaping. The book paradoxically is larger than its teller so that Ishmael's revealed "truths" through statement, metaphor, and analogy serve only to provoke our own quest to translate all the mysterious "markings" he draws attention to; untranslatable finally as the markings on the lid of Queequeg's empty coffin.

I see the book as Melville's grand fiction of order—form, the idea of order itself, is his central thematic concern.

I think Melville, in *Moby-Dick* and elsewhere, is appalled at the obsessive tendency of the more intelligent members of the human race to allegorize life, to project their personal longings and hangups onto the great mysteries of the world.

If my teaching methods were informed by my vision of the book, I suppose I should be less reluctant to leave my students, at least occasionally, "lost in its unshored, harborless immensities." Maybe I'll try it.

I do not want my students so fearful of missing some profound truth that they miss the obvious surface delights of Melville's book.

We can say many important things about the book; what we can not do is finally sum it up. *Moby-Dick* is finally as evasive as Moby Dick.

Like Ishmael, I am eclectic, a multi-valent sensibility ready to employ any means—however subtle or vulgar—to grasp the elusive quarry: an oxymoronic entity which forever haunts those who dare approach it seriously.

I'm a naive bourgeois realist who still believes that literature has a referent to the external world and to my inner life of thought and feeling. Melville's works, especially *Pierre*, may be self-deconstructing and may display blindness and insight, but I feel at home with them now that I've stopped trying to swallow them and let them swallow me.

Most students have untapped reservoirs of response to the individual heroism of Ahab's quest and self-destruction, and to Ishmael's precarious, problematic survival as the dramatically rendered alternative to that self-destruction. This response cannot be elicited readily by an abstract, primarily thematic discussion of the book. I think it is elicited more readily by an appropriate Aristotelian apprehension of the action being imitated by characters on whose behalf we experience pity & fear, along with an awareness of the particular "thought" that gives rise to our pity & fear.

Going into the course, I admit I knew or cared little about Herman Melville. *Moby-Dick* had formerly been misrepresented to me as both a "little kid's book" and "the worst novel ever written." This preconception of mine certainly is not uncommon—teachers of *Moby-Dick* would do well to realize that.

I try to ask open-ended questions which will lead them to the central concerns of the work; this is fairly simple with *Moby-Dick* since everything leads to almost everything else.

The most important thing I do is to let the students discover Melville. To "teach" him ruins the awe and wonder that his writing repeatedly brings. . . . The great risk of this project is that it could try to objectify *M-D*. The last paragraph in "Of the Monstrous Pictures of Whales" offers the caution that is needed whenever we try to fix a way of teaching, or writing about Melville.

The trick is to let the students get angry with Melville, and then to let them discover that those very same features of the book which they take to be arbitrary actually are *dramatically* appropriate for the characters of Ishmael and Ahab.

Students learn how much they can interestingly press the images and ideas in the book. Most of them are good with plot and character already, but *MD* is an especially useful text for revealing that one can pursue in depth the implications of a metaphor, a line of reasoning, or a rhetorical stance. In other words, it is an excellent book for learning how to read well.

Editions

Since a main difficulty reported in teaching *Moby-Dick* is just getting the students to finish it, the choice of a classroom edition can be crucial. While some instructors, sensitive to their students' finances, chose an inexpensive, pocket-size format, the squitchy type and unreliable texts of most such editions make them a false economy. Further, many teachers thought some supplementary material—maps, whaling diagrams, factual notes—enhanced the reading of the book. The three editions discussed below and listed by editor's name in Works Cited seem on the basis of the questionnaires and an examination of all available editions the most viable. For a fuller listing of editions see G. Thomas Tanselle, *A Checklist of Editions of* Moby-Dick, *1851–1976*, which also contains helpful information on the publishing history of the book, as well as photographs and detailed descriptions of the first American and English editions.

The Norton Critical Edition, edited by Harrison Hayford and Hershel Parker, was favored by the most respondents; accuracy of text was the most frequent reason. The textual history of *Moby-Dick* is complex and often conjectural, since neither manuscript nor proofs are extant. Hayford and Parker have shown that the first American edition, which the best previous editors had used as copy-text, needs to be emended and supplemented by the corrections Melville made on the American proofs before they were sent over to England to be reset there. Unfortunately, these authorial corrections have to be winnowed from the British publisher's heavy bowdlerizing and domesticating. More detailed explanations appear in "Textual Problems of *Moby-Dick*" in the Norton edition (471–77) and in Hershel Parker's article "Practical Editions: *Moby-Dick*." The Norton also contains maps of Melville's voyages and that of the *Pequod*, an illustrated account of whaling and whale-craft, relevant reviews and letters by Melville, analogues and sources, selected contemporary reviews and later appraisals, and a well-chosen sampler of modern criticism up to the year of publication. Respondents found this last section the most dispensable, either because they felt the selections need updating or because they prefer not to have their students read outside interpretations. But they were pleased with the nature and amount of annotation: generally factual footnotes sparingly used. The Norton is also the text cited in most recent criticism and scholarship, including this book.

While many teachers were satisfied with the Norton's readability, a significant number preferred Charles Feidelson's edition, published by Bobbs-Merrill, for this very factor, specifying the larger print and wider margins. Although it uses only the American edition as copy-text, it is carefully and intelligently edited. Like the Norton, it has maps and diagrams, and its drawings of whaling vessels are particularly clear. Unlike the Norton, it has extensive interpretive notes as well as factual ones, a feature about which respondents were divided—some chose the book in spite of these notes, while some found them particularly valuable for undergraduates. Several teachers, in fact, use the Bobbs-Merrill for their undergraduate classes and the Norton for their graduate students. Although the interpretations put forth in the footnotes are eminently sane and often incisive, I feel their existence tends to stop student interpretation rather than inspire it and to suggest that all cruxes have somewhere been solved.

Another text that deserves some attention is the Penguin, edited by Harold Beaver. This edition has the advantages of a pocket-size format and readable type, and it builds on—or, some would say, blatantly steals from—the textual work of Hayford and Parker. Beaver feels that the Norton editors were too enamored of the new-found usefulness of the English text, and he restores from the American edition what he sees as functional puns and deliberate roughness. However one may question his judgments, Beaver plays with his cards up, reproducing the Norton list of differences between the American and British editions and tabulating exactly what changes he has adopted. The edition contains a voyage map and a cross section of a whaler, as well as several pages of illustrations, the most valuable of which is a clear reproduction of a Quito doubloon similar to the one described in the novel. That the 280 pages of "Commentary" are consigned to the end of the volume only partially mitigates the drawbacks of this section. Beaver's interpretations are more eccentric and convoluted than Feidelson's, and he seems even more convinced of their rightness.

Instructors were asked to describe what they would like to see in an ideal classroom text, and here is a rough composite sketch: the text of the Norton or of the forthcoming Northwestern-Newberry edition, the print and layout of the Bobbs-Merrill (with a much stronger binding), Melville's review "Hawthorne and His Mosses" and selected letters but no twentieth-century criticism, no footnotes or only factual ones, pertinent maps and diagrams—all at a low price. While we wait for this edition, we should choose from the present ones with care and with our own predilections in mind, since as Millicent Bell argues in the Approaches section below we should be rereading the book each time along with our students.

Critical and Background Reading

Most of the teachers polled assigned little or no outside reading to their undergraduates, some on the practical ground that getting them to read through the novel was challenge enough, some on the philosophical ground that nothing should divert attention from the primary text. Those that did require outside reading most often chose Melville's review "Hawthorne and His Mosses" and the letters written during and immediately after the composition of *Moby-Dick*, especially the long, sometimes manic ones to Hawthorne. Both review and letters, conveniently available in the Norton edition, are so central to an understanding of the book that many teachers who do not use this edition type out long extracts for handouts. Teachers who required or suggested additional student reading most often mention the same titles they recommend as helpful for beginning teachers and those that they themselves consult most frequently, so all three categories will be combined in what follows.

The critical work mentioned most frequently was F. O. Matthiessen, *American Renaissance*. Aside from providing contexts for the entire period, the book has 143 closely set and tightly argued pages on Melville that lay down the major directions for much subsequent scholarly and critical work—the relations with Hawthorne, the influence of Shakespeare, the tragic vision, the economic and social backgrounds. Two other books often mentioned that also have historic as well as intrinsic importance are D. H. Lawrence, *Studies in Classic American Literature*, and Charles Olson, *Call Me Ishmael*. Those that claim both books are eccentric, skewed, often hysterical are probably right, but few critical studies come as close to matching the passionate intensity of their subject. Lawrence, impatient with Melville's conscious philosophizing, is drawn to the novel's depiction of "the sheer naked slidings of the elements" (146), although ironically the English writer offers his own oversimplified symbolic interpretation. Olson, who discovered Melville's set of Shakespeare containing rough notes for *Moby-Dick*, juxtaposes this knowledge with elements of myth, history, and geography to produce a book that has had its own share of critical interpretation.

In addition to Matthiessen, several other works on the entire period, as well as even broader studies of American fiction, were often listed: Charles Feidelson, Jr., *Symbolism and American Literature*; R. W. B. Lewis, *The American Adam*; Richard Chase, *The American Novel and Its Tradition*; Leslie Fiedler, *Love and Death in the American Novel*; Daniel G. Hoffman, *Form and Fable in American Fiction*; Leo Marx, *The Machine in the Garden*; Richard Slotkin, *Regeneration through Violence*; Michael Davitt Bell, *The Development of American Romance*; and John T. Irwin, *American Hieroglyphics*. In general, these books have the defects of their virtues: they provide helpful ways of viewing *Moby-Dick*, in terms of both conceptual handles and American cultural contexts, but their single angles of vision rarely do justice to Melville's multifaceted work.

Several general studies of Melville provide the inclusiveness and subtlety often missing in the books just mentioned. A rich chapter in Newton Arvin's *Herman Melville*, for example, analyzes *Moby-Dick* on four levels—literal, oneiric, moral, and mythic—and gives the language of the book the detailed attention it deserves. Warner Berthoff, *The Example of Melville*, examines the use of words in even more detail and extends the analysis of Melville's distinctive qualities as a writer to paragraphs, chapters, and the entire career. In *Melville's Thematics of Form*, Edgar Dryden sees *Moby-Dick* as the culmination of Melville's developing interest in self-conscious forms and in fiction as the only available truth. Other studies of Melville regularly listed were William Ellery Sedgwick, *Herman Melville: The Tragedy of Mind*; Richard Chase, *Herman Melville: A Critical Study*; Ronald Mason, *The Spirit above the Dust*; Lawrance Thompson, *Melville's Quarrel with God*; Edward H. Rosenberry, *Melville and the Comic Spirit*; Milton R. Stern, *The Fine Hammered Steel of Herman Melville*; Merlin Bowen, *The Long Encounter*; James E. Miller, Jr., *A Reader's Guide to Herman Melville*; John Seelye, *Melville: The Ironic Diagram*; Rowland A. Sherrill, *The Prophetic Melville*; Carolyn L. Karcher, *Shadow over the Promised Land: Slavery, Race and Violence in Melville's America*; and Joyce Sparer Adler, *War in Melville's Imagination*. Since the questionnaires were received, two other books on Melville have appeared; like the last two mentioned above, they integrate critical readings of Melville's work with the political and social contexts of his time: Michael Paul Rogin, *Subversive Genealogy: The Politics and Art of Herman Melville*, and James Duban, *Melville's Major Fiction: Politics, Theology, and Imagination*. Also two books in which Melville divides the attention with Hawthorne are valuable: Richard Brodhead, *Hawthorne, Melville, and the Novel*, is an excellent genre—or rather mixed-genre—study, and Sharon Cameron, *The Corporeal Self*, views *Moby-Dick*'s central concern as the physical boundaries of the self. Three books on nineteenth-century literature that cross the Atlantic to provide rich perspectives on Melville's work are Walter L. Reed, *Meditations on the Hero: A Study of the Romantic Hero in Nineteenth-Century Fiction*; Edwin Eigner, *The Metaphysical Novel in England and America: Dickens, Bulwer, Hawthorne, Melville;* and David Simpson, *Fetishism and Imagination: Dickens, Melville, Conrad.*

When Harry Levin wrote that "the investigation of *Moby-Dick* might almost be said to have taken the place of whaling among the industries of New England" (vi), he was only slightly exaggerating, so it would be difficult to list here even the important articles. The following, though, deserve mention for their frequent appearance on the questionnaires: Henry A. Murray, "In nomine diaboli," both a personal account of his love affair with the book and a reading in Freudian terms; Walter E. Bezanson, "*Moby-Dick*: Work of Art," an eloquent essay, the significance of which for subsequent criticism is described in the first paragraph of the Milder essay in the Approaches section; James Dean Young, "The Nine Gams of the *Pequod*," an earnest attempt to relate structure to theme; George R. Stewart, "The Two *Moby-Dicks*," sets forth the theory developed also by Leon Howard and Howard P. Vincent that the book was written in two stages, a fairly simple sea story drastically transformed by Melville's encounters with Shakespeare, Hawthorne, and his own deepest self (this thesis should be approached only with the cautions and additional information offered by Milder in "The Composition of *Moby-Dick*"); Joseph A. Ward, "The Function of the Cetological Chapters in *Moby-Dick*," which has been to some extent superseded by Robert M. Greenberg, "Cetology: Center of Multiplicity and Discord in *Moby-Dick*"; Howard C. Horsford, "The Design of the Argument in *Moby-Dick*," a perceptive interrelation of intellectual context to narrative; Harrison Hayford, "Unnecessary Duplicates," an alternative theory about the composition of the book, based on internal evidence. Convenient collections of essays that reprint several of the articles above are Tyrus Hillway and Luther S. Mansfield, eds., Moby-Dick *Centennial Essays*; Milton R. Stern, ed., *Discussions of* Moby-Dick; Richard Chase, ed., *Melville: A Collection of Critical Essays*; Howard P. Vincent, ed., *Charles E. Merrill Studies in* Moby-Dick; Michael T. Gilmore, ed., *Twentieth Century Interpretations of* Moby-Dick. Journals have devoted entire issues to Melville—*ESQ* no. 28, pt. 3 (1962), *Modern Fiction Studies* 8.3 (1962), and *Studies in the Novel* 1.4 (1969)—and *College Literature* has published an issue exclusively on *Moby-Dick* (2.3 [1975]).

Book-length studies of *Moby-Dick* provide more sea room both for more inclusive insights and also for submerging the text in one's own vision. William S. Gleim offers a Swedenborgian interpretation in *The Meaning of* Moby-Dick, and M. O. Percival gives a more workable Kierkegaardian one in *A Reading of* Moby-Dick. Two more recent books use their interpretive schemes more productively: Edward Edinger, *Melville's* Moby-Dick: *A Jungian Commentary*, which in treating the book as a dream misses the ways Melville analyzes his myths himself, and Bainard Cowan, *Exiled Waters*, a study in the historical tradition of allegory. Still the two major books are Paul Brodtkorb, *Ishmael's White World*, and Robert Zoellner, *The Salt-Sea Mastodon*. Aside from their intellectual energy, the two have little in common: Brodtkorb's phenomenological approach emphasizes the elusiveness of meaning and the ways in which an anxious narrator tries to frame formlessness, while Zoellner's more conventional approach fits theme and imagery together in coherent patterns. If Brodtkorb has a fault it is that of projecting his method onto the book as a thematic concern, so that Melville or Ishmael end up with insights remarkably similar to those of, say, Heidegger; if Zoellner has one it is in wrapping the book up too neatly, especially by asking us to accept Ishmael and reject Ahab. Despite these reservations, one could hardly do better, given a short time to prepare, than to read one or both of these books.

Two theoretical studies of the modern novel give us more sophisticated ways of viewing the relations between Ishmael's narration and Ahab's story. James Guetti, *The Limits of Metaphor*, sees the two as complementary: "Without Ahab as potential seer the unstructured artifice of the narrative would be indicative of aimless complexity; without Ahab as monomaniac the complexity would be destroyed by a simplifying moment of vision" (110–11). Building on Guetti's work, Bruce F. Kawin, *The Mind of the Novel*, shows how a vision of the ineffable (Ahab's) turns into self-reflexive discourse when Ishmael tries to embody it in words.

Many teachers reported the value of close readings with their students, especially as a way of introducing them early to the complexities of style, voice, theme. Fortunately, if we apply this method to the opening of the novel, there are four excellent analyses already published, each from a different perspective. Warwick Wadlington in "Ishmael's Godly Gamesomeness: Selftaste and Rhetoric in *Moby-Dick*" points out the dialectic in the first chapter between engagement and distance, self-loss and self-consolidation, that occurs on both the plane of Ishmael and his materials and that of the reader and the text. David Leverenz in his psychoanalytic study of the book shows how the syntax of the first paragraph reveals psychic conflicts in the narrator. In "'Loomings': Yarns and Figures in the Fabric," Harrison Hayford focuses on Ishmael's character to reveal images and motifs that weave their way through the entire book. James Nechas's linguistic analysis of the opening draws attention to Melville's use of the negative throughout the work.

Of articles specifically related to teaching the book, Stephen Black, "On Reading Psychoanalytically" stands out for its theoretical clarity and its effective use of "The Try-Works" as an illustration of method. Also helpful are Gordon Roper, "On Teaching *Moby-Dick*"; Merton M. Sealts, Jr., "Approaching Melville through 'Hawthorne and His Mosses'"; Paul McCarthy, "A Note on Teaching *Moby-Dick*"; and Terence Martin, *Teaching a Novel: Moby-Dick in the Classroom*.

The range and number of background and specialized studies on Melville's work give a sense of his restless intellectual curiosity and his complex eclecticism. The single most important such study for *Moby-Dick* is Howard P. Vincent, *The Trying-Out of Moby-Dick*. Although Vincent attempts a complete investigation into the origins of the book, the part that has proved most valuable is his account of Melville's borrowings from his "numerous fish documents," especially the five primary books he used for fact and color about whaling. Other helpful background studies are William Braswell, *Melville's Religious Thought*; Nathalia Wright, *Melville's Use of the Bible*; Henry F. Pommer, *Milton and Melville*; Gerard M. Sweeney, *Melville's Use of Classical Mythology*; T. Walter Herbert, Moby-Dick *and Calvinism*; and Maria Ujházy, *Herman Melville's World of Whaling*. James Baird, *Ishmael*, examines Melville in the context of "primitivism" (broadly defined here as the rejection of traditional religious symbols for more individually shaped ones), while H. Bruce Franklin, *The Wake of the Gods*, shows Melville's theoretical and practical interests in the mythography of his time. These myth studies can be supplemented by Dorothee M. Finkelstein, *Melville's Orienda*, a study of Melville's use of Near Eastern sources, and H. B. Kulkarni, *Moby-Dick: A Hindu Avatar*, which is not as farfetched as its title suggests. Perry Miller, *The Raven and the Whale*, is a lively if not always accurate account of the literary cliques and squabbles in Melville's New York. Thomas Farel Heffernan, *Stove by a Whale*, reprints in full Owen Chase's account of the sinking of the *Essex*, a book that much fired Melville's imagination. Two background articles worth noting are Millicent Bell, "Pierre Bayle and *Moby-Dick*," and Thomas Vargish, "Gnostic *Mythos* in *Moby-Dick*."

While teachers should undoubtedly be as familiar as possible with all these backgrounds and contexts, how much they should bring into the classroom is an open question. To take one example, Perry Miller in the book mentioned above discusses the political and social implications of the ingredients Ishmael and Queequeg find in their chowder in the chapter of that name, showing how the particular recipe places Melville on one side of a heated but now forgotten literary debate about native traditions versus refinement. Whether this knowledge actually enhances or diminishes a student's experience of the text, his or her ability imaginatively to re-create the tastes, smells, atmosphere of the scene, is another matter. The novel itself revels in pedantry and delights in its plenitude even as it underscores its own limits and pretensions. As David Leverenz and Jane Mushabac point out below, we teachers have to be sharp and sensitive enough to realize when our own learning becomes a defense against the open exploration of what we do not as yet know.

Biography, Reference, Bibliography

Leon Howard's *Herman Melville: A Biography* is still considered the most accurate and thorough biography; it should be used with its companion work,

Jay Leyda, *The Melville Log*, which contains the sources and documentation on which Howard's narrative is based. To help those pressed for time, Howard has also written a concise pamphlet for the University of Minnesota series, *Herman Melville*, and Hershel Parker provides an even more concise and up-to-date biographical sketch in *The Norton Anthology of American Literature*. For more detailed accounts of Melville's childhood and youth, see William H. Gilman, *Melville's Early Life and* Redburn, and Walter Herbert, Jr., Moby-Dick *and Calvinism*. Charles Anderson's pioneering study, *Melville in the South Seas*, follows his life still further. Melville's granddaughter Eleanor Metcalf provides some fresh biographical data, primarily from family papers, in *Herman Melville: Cycle and Epicycle*. A book of particular interest for those interested in Melville and American literary history is Merton M. Sealts, Jr., *The Early Lives of Melville: Nineteenth Century Biographical Sketches and Their Authors*. Biographical studies from more specialized perspectives are Edwin H. Miller, *Melville*, a sometimes provocative but overly speculative psychobiography, and Michael Rogin, *Subversive Genealogy*, an attempt to link the political and social milieu of the time with Melville's family dynamics. We still need a wide-ranging, inclusive study charting Melville's spiritual and intellectual growth, but in the meantime, the best source is *The Letters of Herman Melville*, edited by Merrell R. Davis and William H. Gilman.

Probably the single most handy reference work is Moby-Dick *as Doubloon*, ed. Hershel Parker and Harrison Hayford. This book conveniently reprints in full most of the contemporary reviews of *Moby-Dick*; a few that were discovered later appear in Hershel Parker, "Five Reviews Not in Moby-Dick *as Doubloon*." These reviews are important not only because Melville's reading of them affected his artistic course but also because they illuminate the reading conventions and expectations of Melville's audience. Other sections document the relative critical neglect during Melville's later life and the three decades after his death, the beginnings of the Melville revival in the early 1920s, and the range of modern responses to the book. The snippets, though, are so fragmentary and numerous that depth is often elusive. Two other collections tracing Melville's reputation and sampling critical responses to his work are Hershel Parker, ed., *The Recognition of Herman Melville*, and Watson G. Branch, ed., *Melville: The Critical Heritage*. Another almost indispensable book is the Hendricks House edition of *Moby-Dick*, edited by Luther S. Mansfield and Howard P. Vincent. The 269 pages of explanatory notes are filled with helpful information, especially about the literary and whaling sources. This book is difficult to find, but it is still in print and available from the publisher (Hendricks House, Inc., Main St., Putney, VT 05346). It is important also because the more readable and usable of the two computer-assisted concordances to *Moby-Dick*, the one edited by Eugene Irey, is based on this text. Another tool that has served Melville scholars well is Merton M. Sealts, Jr., *Melville's Reading: A Check-List of Books Owned and Borrowed.*

The two best starting places for bibliographical information are the annotated bibliography in Parker and Hayford, Moby-Dick *as Doubloon*, and Nathalia Wright's chapter on Melville in James Woodress, ed., *Eight American Authors.* Since neither goes beyond 1969, they need to be supplemented by the Melville chapter in the annual *American Literary Studies*, traditionally one of the most perceptive chapters in the book, written by a series of canny Melvillians—Willard Thorp, Merton Sealts, Hershel Parker, and Robert Milder. Also helpful in bringing the Melville bibliography up to date are Claude Hunsberger, "Vectors in Recent *Moby-Dick* Criticism," and the columns of *Melville Society Extracts*, especially for news of current and forthcoming work. Other bibliographical volumes are Theodore L. Gross and Stanley Wertheim, *Hawthorne, Melville, Stephen Crane;* Beatrice Ricks and Joseph Adams, *Herman Melville: A Reference Bibliography;* Brian Higgins, *Herman Melville: An Annotated Bibliography, Volume 1: 1846–1930;* Jeanetta Boswell, *Herman Melville and the Critics;* and John Bryant, *Melville Dissertations, 1924–1980.*

Aids to Teaching

Although *Moby-Dick* supplies much of its own background material, many teachers also use visual aids to help make the book more accessible to the intellect and imagination. The illustrative material in the Norton, Bobbs-Merrill, and Penguin editions can be supplemented by the many excellent woodcuts in the Arion Press edition, made more widely available by the University of California Press in 1981. Since the bookmaker decided not to depict characters or dramatic incidents, the illustrator, Barry Moser, turns his talents primarily to scenes and diagrams of whales and whalings. Many instructors reported finding useful photographs of whales in the *National Geographic* and the *National Wildlife Magazine* (see especially the June-July 1975 issue). Another useful source of illustrations is the picture biography, Gay Wilson Allen, *Melville and His World.*

The single most helpful film is *A Whaling Voyage*, a half-hour condensation of a 1922 silent feature *Down to the Sea in Ships*, which includes shots of the Whaleman's Bethel in New Bedford and faithfully re-creates nineteenth-century methods of chasing, killing, and trying out whales. The condensation can be rented from the Educational Development Center (55 Chapel St., Newton, MA 02160). Two other half-hour films, *Herman Melville: November in My Soul* and *Herman Melville: Consider the Sea* provide glimpses of Melvillian settings—Arrowhead, harbors and whaling ships, and present readings from the works with appropriate visuals. The latter, narrated by Richard Wilbur, is more satisfying as a film, the former more informative about Melville's life and cultural milieu. Both of the films are more effective than the typical lecture on the same materials, but one also has to weigh the value of passive absorption against that of active student participation. Still, the short length of all three films allows some class time afterward for discussion.

There is widespread agreement among the questionnaire respondents that the 1956 Warner Brothers film of *Moby-Dick*, casting Gregory Peck as Ahab and something like the Goodyear Blimp as the whale, is unsatisfying. Milton R. Stern, however, ingeniously shows in "The Whale and the Minnow: *Moby-Dick* and the Movies" how a comparison of the film (now available in videocassette format) with the book can highlight the nature and strengths of the latter.

The most effective aids are the least transferable; many instructors bring in their own favorite posters of sailing ships, cartoons and other materials from popular culture, recorded songs by and about whales, pasteboard whales—materials less important for what they actually teach than for conveying the teacher's own enthusiasm and immersion in the subject. And it is even more effective to involve the students in collecting or creating this material. One of my own favorite assignments is to have the students draw the painting in the entry of the Spouter Inn that Ishmael verbally describes and then say what this exercise tells them about the ways Melville's narrator uses his mind and his language.

Part Two

APPROACHES

INTRODUCTION

The essays in this part are divided into two sections, "Approaching the Text" and "The Classroom Situation," but the categories are not watertight or mutually exclusive: our sense of the text and the way we see it interacting with the reader will shape our teaching. Millicent Bell's view of reading as primarily sequential and temporal creates a teaching situation focusing on process, on students' immediate reaction to what they have just read in or before class. Bell would not insist, as many other instructors do, that students finish *Moby-Dick* before the first class discussion. Her view of the book and how it should be read obviates a device often mentioned by other teachers—the introductory lecture on the contexts of the novel, on Melville's life and times, on what students can or should expect. In contrast, William Shurr's understanding of the book is more spatial and generic. His reading makes sense primarily after the novel is finished and relies on information that the instructor will probably have to provide to the student—for example, the classical forms of tragedy and comedy, the relation of Calvinism to American cultural history. He offers a structure that he admits may be too neat but that oversimplifies only in the service of giving the student an initial approach to the book that can subsequently be complicated and refined. Robert Milder's long essay mediates these two positions in arguing that Melville discovered the form of his work in the act of composing it. As Milder suggests, his essay is addressed more to the questions we would ask ourselves before we teach the book than to those we bring into the classroom to ask the students. While acknowledging the complexity and elusiveness of Melville's form, his reading does allow us to explore with the students more traditional questions about themes, genres, and coherence.

These three essays will help the teacher new to *Moby-Dick* in another way: although each puts forth a fresh and individual reading of the book, all three encompass and synthesize some of the best in recent critical thinking. Milder in particular places the book quickly but not reductively in contexts such as Melville's career, the American line of retrospective narration "in which the story of the hero is . . . assimilated to the broader story of the narrator's own life," and the nonfiction works of the American Renaissance. Shurr's emphasis on Calvinism, which sets the stage for the classroom encounters that Verduin describes later, recapitulates some of the important work done in the field of American studies. Bell makes vividly immediate the often abstract work of reader-response theorists and of phenomenological critics who have written on the book.

Although the Cowan and Marovitz articles were written independently, they complement each other well. Both authors see *Moby-Dick* not as personally or nationally idiosyncratic but as an incorporation and rereading of keystone texts in the Western tradition. While Cowan's article is more theoretical and speculative, Marovitz details the assignments, procedures, and schedules of his classroom teaching. Both essays show how the novel's vast scope can be turned to educational advantage instead of serving as one more excuse to bewail the unpreparedness of our students, and they suggest ways—other than the merely chronological—of organizing and focusing readings historically.

Axelrod's ambitious article relates a theory of the book to the actual practice of teaching it to nonmajors. Like Cowan and Marovitz, Axelrod views the problems of the teaching situation—in this case the lack of an interpretive community—as opportunities rather than oppressions. Verduin and Leverenz are also concerned with specific student communities—in the first instance, religious; in the second, economic and ideological. Both essays suggest the importance of knowing what our students bring to the book and show that we can best find this out not by chatting with them after class or reading sociological studies but by opening the classroom to immediate personal responses and listening well. These two essays make it clear that although we may find some student responses more valuable or relevant than others, every response, if examined sensitively, yields some usable information on the transaction between the text and one reader's mind. Further, by delineating the assumptions and backgrounds they themselves bring to the book, Verduin and Leverenz gives us a rich sense of how the classroom can be a stage for intense and illuminating interactions among text, students, and teacher. The question is not whether our own and our students' personal, affective factors should enter into the classroom; these factors operate in any case, and what matters is how we probe, harness, and clarify them.

The oxymoron in Bergstrom's title, "open structures," and the related paradox Bergstrom describes near the beginning of his essay are central to this volume, especially to the five essays following his. The responses to the questionnaires reveal a gap in the ways we teach. Philosophically, most of us buy into the Ishmaelean virtues of free and open inquiry, of surrendering, at least momentarily, our own stabilities to try on other ways of seeing. But in our classrooms we find ourselves adopting the Ahabian strategies of maintaining tight control, centering all interactions on ourselves, and moving only on the straight iron way of our own interpretation or syllabus. We also know, though, that mere anarchy does not work. It is easy to be merely negative, to oppose authoritarianism, rigidity, foreclosure, but it is difficult to create settings and structures in which students can speak openly and productively to themselves and to the teacher. Bergstrom and some of the other contributors have created such structures and have used them effectively in their own classrooms. The structures, though, are presented here not to be adopted wholesale by other teachers but as models of the strategies we can construct for our own students and ourselves. Bergstrom was one of the many instructors who along with their questionnaires sent in detailed study guides, intelligent mappings of patterns in the book, and other classroom heuristics. None of these materials is reproduced here, for fear that other teachers might just reduplicate it and hand it out in their classrooms without going through the processes of close reading and complex organization that originally produced it and that make it viable in working with students.

The teaching stances of Bergstrom, Sten, Mushabac, Wolff, Crichton, and Wallace, then, are offered as exemplary, not as prescriptive or easily transferable. The first three suggest how a variety of insights and methods can come together fruitfully in a teaching of the book. The last three present relatively specialized approaches that comprise only a portion of each teacher's actual in-class treatment of the book. These approaches—through the concepts of lexicon and of mythic space and through the paintings of Turner—do suggest, though, some ways a teacher can break set, can make the strange familiar—and vice versa. They suggest further that the limits of our discipline are arbitrary and often self-imposed.

To return to a point raised in the preface, I want to underscore that several of the teachers here emphasize frequent informal student writing, especially in the form of journals. As Wallace says in his article, this mode is particularly relevant to teaching *Moby-Dick*: "A journal not only forces students to crystallize their own responses as they read but also builds into the learning process an emphasis on process itself." Empirical studies and the best educational and literary theories suggest that students do not really make knowledge their own unless they themselves articulate it. Further, writing for each class session deepens discussion significantly; the students arrive with a certain commitment to their ideas, which they have explored and formulated more fully than usual. The reason many of us do not assign the amount of writing we know we should is that we also feel a strange compulsion to grade—to evaluate, copyedit, "correct"—every word each student writes. In feeling this we not only generate a huge amount of work for ourselves, we divert attention from the novel's own emphasis on writing as a way of making personal sense out of experience, of probing and ordering its flux, of measuring verbal abstractions against our own felt life. Also, as teachers we tend to make those assignments we feel comfortable in evaluating, such as critical analyses, and to avoid the more open-ended kinds of writing that bring us to the heart of such issues.

A related strategy, mentioned on several of the best questionnaire responses and elaborated here by Marovitz and Crichton, is to have the students supply the background material and contexts instead of automatically turning to our yellowed lecture notes. Again, the particular facts the students uncover will not be as important as making them aware of the process of fact-finding, one of the thematic concerns of *Moby-Dick*. Leverenz and Bergstrom provide further useful suggestions on how one then examines and evaluates the facts showing students that what we do not know about this book is at least as important as what we do.

This insight reduces the danger that the teacher new to *Moby-Dick* may be intimidated by the vast knowledge that, ideally, one should possess to teach the book, as implied particularly by the essays of Milder, Cowan, Marovitz, and Sten and by the very bulk of titles in the Materials section, which itself is only a skeletal list of resources. As Bell, Mushabac, and Leverenz suggest, a teacher can do just as well—if not better—with a spirit of tough-minded openness, an immediate responsiveness to the students' transactions with the text, a collaborative sense of sharing in the endless activities of fact-finding and interpreting. Finally—and this word has never quite been the same since Ishmael used it to begin his famous closing paragraph of "Cetology," emphasizing the virtues and necessity of inconclusiveness—we must learn to teach this book in the moment-to-moment life of the classroom, with the help and resistance of students, those other minds that keep our own in perpetual tack. The present volume is but a moored beginning.

MB

APPROACHING THE TEXT
Flux and Form

The Indeterminate *Moby-Dick*

Millicent Bell

To "teach" a long fiction is too often to deny its indeterminateness, its plurality, its mystery. A tradition of over-confident explication still urges us to suggest, in the classroom, that everything could be explained if only there were time enough and to offer at least a map of interpretation, a straight path through the woods of difficult works. Our conscientiousness insists that we give our students the benefit of our own hard-earned understanding, the fruit of repeated readings and reflection and of the assimilation of others' criticism. We know that we cannot safely reduce complexity, and we try to account for self-contradiction as structured ambiguity and irony. But a class hour may be all we have to resolve contradictions into some pattern. We are too likely to sacrifice—for ourselves and for our students—the acknowledgment of doubt, of irreducibility, and our and their negative capability as readers.

Teaching may, however, provide teachers with an opportunity to regain this capability for themselves as they cherish it in their students. In the company of students they reperceive the lost text they once encountered. They may discover that even the most closed of structures possesses an openness, in the sense of a resistance to resolved interpretation, and that this resistance, which seems to grow less with rereading and study, is a feature of the work that should not be forgotten. Readers who think they have solved all the puzzles, arrived at all the answers to questions of meaning, perhaps no longer read: those who win to the last page after travail and error and grow in understanding without surrendering doubt are themselves heroes of the work they have experienced. They have been educated by experience along with the fictional hero—as in the representative novel of education—and look back, finally, at the past as a succession of states.

It is perfectly true that literary works deserve repeated readings and that each reading is different. Many modern works in particular ask for the foreknowledge from which a second reading benefits. But after the first reading we organize the various elements and effects we have encountered in a way it has long been customary to call "spatial"; indeed, we even begin the process as we read for the first time, tentatively arranging the unfinished accumulation of impressions as they take their places in our minds, seeing them in a simultaneity of recall. At the end we become aware of designs of symmetry, rhythm, contrast, or repetition in the whole that may be apprehended at once. But it is well to remember that the spatialization of fiction is the work of our memory, which brings together in a single vision what happened early and late. The experience of literature—which is closer to music than to painting—is something else. The first reading especially, unaided by foreknowledge, is valid as the purest condition of the *Nacheinander* of storytelling, however valid additionally are later rereadings. Fiction is after all a time art. While it may present us with life at a standstill or life on the run, it must itself inevitably put one foot—that is, one word—after another and transpire in time, as painting does not. In abstracting total form, trying to see as coexisting what have come to us as successive impressions, we tend to forget that the novel is a process that changes us as we grow minutely older.

I particularly feel the need of such reminders when, as I repeatedly have for many years, I face up to the difficulties and opportunities of discussing *Moby-Dick* in the classroom. Today, of course, one is encouraged to acknowledge that there may be many interpretations for literary works—perhaps as many as there are readers, to take the most extreme relativist stand. Even if one refuses to go this far in dissolving the boundaries set by the object on the page, there is greater readiness now to allow for the polysemous qualities of literature. But I confess to having always felt an incapacity to close certain books with a confident critical summary. I put the word "teach" in quotation marks at the start of these remarks because it implies that the teacher holds something complete that he or she is going to make over to others or help them discover, like the body of information and explanation they might acquire in a course in organic chemistry or Roman history. To teach literary works in this sense is to treat texts as textbooks from which something is to be extracted, something called meaning that floats there in the classroom as one talks and must be captured and set down in the notebook. But the literary text is, in fact, not to be left behind, a mere reference tool, in this way; it is the beginning *and* end of reading, an activity that can never be exactly summarized, that can only be repeated, that does not exist as knowledge apart from itself. It is a process that we can only know in the doing and that our teaching is simply designed to make more profound.

And so teachers must be content simply to promote without in any way reducing this sense of process that accompanies the reading on which they launch their students. *Moby-Dick* requires more than one class meeting, certainly, during which teacher and students may come as close as they can to the impossible ideal of reading every bit of it aloud together; together they need to go at a pace that at least enables them to exchange the reflections of explorers or hunters stopping by stages to take note of where they are. These meetings should be a series during which one goes through the book without gun or compass till one confronts the great bear or, to take the image from Melville instead of Faulkner, discards the quadrant in the hunt for the great whale. One may be particularly justified in inviting undirected response to *Moby-Dick* since Melville's work is so notoriously polysemous. One need not make students feel that critical commentary is forbidden fruit, but it is well to remark that the variety of interpretations already made is really an encouragement to individual response: no one need fear that he or she is missing the irrefutable consensus of informed opinion. I try not to refer at the start to the critical controversies myself, not to rob the students too promptly of their innocence of the arguments of the doctors and of their readiness to trust themselves. Innocence of response is particularly needful in this situation—in fact, I hope rather to borrow some from my students, as I have said, than to infect them, prematurely, with my own sophistication.

One may even urge one's students to be more innocent than they already are. For there is no such thing, even for the most inexperienced readers, as an entirely innocent reading; from the beginning they arrive programmed with preconceptions built out of the epistemes of their culture. The meaning of narrative is rooted for them in their sense, as members of the society they inhabit, of cause and effect in human affairs or of the nature of personality, which in or out of fiction is called character. These assumptions operate even if the students have never before read a novel. Their preconceptions of design and meaning are part of their sense of life as well as of literature, which pretends to mimic life. If few will have escaped reading some stories, some novels of one kind or another, none will have escaped exposure to the narrative structures implicit in the way even news is summarized in printed or aural-visual media, not to speak of the flood of narrative forms that pours into consciousness from television and movie screens. First-time readers will, in any case, have enough to do to keep themselves open to a book that frustrates even their most elementary expectations by discontinuous plot and inconsistent narrative voice, by philosophical and factual matter that seems to interrupt the story arbitrarily, by character and symbol that refuse to stay put but float forward from meaning to meaning as the pages pass, by themes that subtly alter with the progress of the other ingredients. These readers will be tempted to blame the author for making reading difficult and for thwarting their elementary ideas of genre—a thwarting that only increases as they develop a sense of literary kinds, for in the end the most sophisticated give over the attempt to assign the book firmly to one category (novel, epic, anatomy, or something else) and say that it has something of them all. What ends in doubt should begin in it, for otherwise we encourage students to select ingredients to meet some scheme that excludes other elements that are not to be ignored if the students are to respect their own sensations.

Meanwhile, teachers must reread with suspended judgment the familiar text lest they mistake memory for the past reality. They must be as uncertain again as their students who have yet to arrive at those explanations of Ahab's monomania or the symbolism of the whale that will be set down with such positiveness (alas!) on the final examination papers. Only so can they participate in the life of the book, moving down the stream in the direction of its flow until they reach Melville's "Finis." It may sound like regression to the method of the lower grades to say, "for tomorrow we will read the first three chapters, and for the next class the next three," as though we give up the hope that the best students might race to the end and be prepared to talk about the book as a whole when class discussion begins. But there can be advantage to our bridling these most eager ones a bit with "let's take it easy; let's see precisely what each stretch appears to be when we meet it and then what the next part means to us; let's make no final definitions just yet; there will be time to test later the fit of general interpretations." Of course, as the successive impressions accumulate, more and more general theories about the whole propose themselves. But, gently, gently—for as E. M. Forster warned years ago, our analytic summaries of meanings are only "a symbol for the book if we want one . . . they do not carry us much further than the acceptance of the book as a yarn—perhaps they carry us backwards, for they may mislead us into harmonizing the incidents, and so losing their roughness and richness" (128). *Moby-Dick* has a roughness and a richness that must not be smoothed down. The wisely passive reader must submit to the flow of its variations of effect and by close attentiveness hope to discover what Melville is about.

By reading in such a mood they will find that they can accept rather than resist the rule of diversity that seems to govern Melville's procedure. It is, indeed, a case of steering by the log and the line so that we submit to the voyage that seems to go swift or slow so arbitrarily. Our students' elementary expectation of narrative progress is the first of their own charts that proves useless. What kind of a story is this, they begin to ask, which seems, for so many pages, to get absolutely nowhere? In one sense the action of *Moby-Dick* must progress continually forward as the *Pequod* moves always onward towards its fate. But the description of that voyage also reproduces the experience of the sailor who is occupied with his duties and concerns on board the ship and is as stationary with respect to it as though he were on land—even more so by virtue of the extreme limitations of space to which he is confined. The sailor has surrendered his personal direction to the ship as to some destinal force over which he has no control. Ishmael is a humble member of the crew, who does not even presume to counsel the captain as the ship is driven ever onward by Ahab's propulsive will. It is this condition that the reader shares, passive, suspended in the unchanging world of the ship. The occupations of its daily round, mat making or blubber boiling as well as the routines of hunting lesser whales than Moby Dick, are represented in the static elements of the book, along with Ishmael's ruminating reflections. Is this stop-and-go pace a denial of progress in the work, a negation of narrative design? Yes it is. But maybe it is supposed to be. Perhaps the very idea of linearity, the idea that life gets anywhere, that there is any meaning to the movement that takes us from one moment to the next, is put under suspicion by a cheerful frustration of our initial conceptions of narrative progress. Ishmael's occupations, his reflections, unsituated in time, even designed to "pass the time" so that we take no note of it, may be a structural equivalent of his view of life, so different from Ahab's. He seems to see himself as confined to the distractions of all men borne unconsciously along by the inscrutable. Ahab, on the other hand, is acutely conscious of time—"even now I lose time," he must say to the captain of the *Rachel* (435; ch. 128). He has the conviction that he shapes experience into a sequence that attains an end. He has the sense of an ending, the compulsion toward apocalypse. But opposed to this commitment to linearity is Ishmael's focus on a still center: the center of consciousness, the witnessing point of view that turns ultimately only on itself and is all that survives the disastrous search.

A readiness to take the book as it comes, disjunctive and diverse as it seems, will assist students in meeting the stylistic mixture of *Moby-Dick*, though already they may ask whether they are reading story or essay and whether they are in the same narrative hands in one part as in another. Of course, the teacher knows the novel of mixed style has precedent in the history of the novel from *Tom Jones* to *Ulysses*, but we have tended to pay attention to fiction that reinforces coherence by adopting a consistent mode and by choosing a voice that if not always a point of view in the Jamesian sense is at least a unifying linguistic perspective. Melville seems to begin in the most comfortable way by employing an identifiable first person, but then this charming narrator, in whom our students will have begun to take keen interest, will be allowed to slip out of view and his voice to become so impersonal as to make us doubt that he is still present. We may want to hold on to the idea that Ishmael is really always around—"I, Ishmael, was one of that crew; my shouts had gone up with the rest," he reminds us after the dramatic "Midnight; Forecastle" chapter (155; ch. 41). But it is well to admit that discontinuity is felt, that the narrator seems to have dropped out of the picture so that we have lost the fixed responsive viewpoint he presented.

Reading so acceptingly we will be less prone to reduce all to a single note, whether of realism or of symbolism—a prime issue in all discussions of this work. The book begins as a realistic adventure tale and goes on to become something else—we professors know that long ago George Stewart showed that this shift might be the result of Melville's mid-passage change of plan. The young author of *Typee, Omoo, Redburn, White-Jacket* began another semiautobiographical sea story and after a while, for reasons ultimately unfathomable (was it reading Shakespeare or meeting Hawthorne that did it? Or some obscure personal arrival at the "inmost leaf of the bulb" [Hayford and Parker 560]?), scrapped it in favor of an excursion into fundamental questions of godhead, being, good and evil, and humanity's place and posture. Since we think we discern this compositional history shall we say that we have caught Melville in default of the final integrative act? Is *Moby-Dick* a work of confused purpose, unresolved contradictions?

Perhaps we can put our bewilderment to a better use than to support the theory of incomplete revision. Reading without prejudice we may find no such break as the theory suggests. We seem to start with candid realism, and so we ignore—not because it is not there but because the narrator does not alert us to watch for it—the loomings of symbolism in the first twenty-two chapters. Yet if we wish we may pause on the simplest things, like the opening "Call me Ishmael," and ask ourselves what the narrator's refusal to give his real name means. Someone may suggest that it is a gesture toward an old pseudorealist guarantee—the pretense by the narrator (who must therefore seem to be a real person) that he must conceal his identity because he does not want to be held accountable for his tale in the real world, like the criminal "whom we will call John" who is interviewed in silhouette on television. But someone else may recognize that this uncommon biblical name has a symbolic and representative function—perhaps the speaker is *an* Ishmael, or the representative of all Ishmaels. And by his asking us to name him, does he not suggest that we also are the authors of the story he tells, that it is at the disposition of human imagination, a fiction? This argument cannot be resolved, and we hold to a prudent irresolution for we can never, even later on, be sure that we are in either the world of fact or that of symbolic fantasy.

With the "six-inch chapter [that] is the stoneless grave of Bulkington" (97; ch. 23), the forward movement of the narrative is halted, and what have seemed jesting by-the-by notes of extraliteral meaning become portentous. "In landlessness alone resides the highest truth": *now* we recall Ishmael's musing about the motives of water-gazers (which we took humorously at the time); now we take with sudden seriousness his revelation (which sounded like a joke) that seagoing was his substitute for pistol and ball. But the effect of our initial impression when we read these passages is not erased by this retrospective realization. Though loomings of symbolism about sea and land and whales had been present, though early enough the ambiguous parable of Jonah as told by Father Mapple suggested that this new story of a man and a whale may be a parable too, still, the authority of fact has been strongly asserted in the New Bedford and Nantucket chapters by a narrator alertly observant of appearances, readily engaged in action. And fact remains a significant, resistant quality in whatever follows. Only now our nerves are tuned to other resonances; fact cannot hereafter sound purely for us. We are ready for the way in the chapter called "Brit," Melville's narrator, presumably still Ishmael, drifts into a consideration of the opposed qualities of land and sea. When in "The Symphony," just at the last moment, the "air smells . . . as if it blew from a faraway meadow" as Ahab gazes downward over the side, we need little besides the description to evoke the accumulated senses of "sea" and "land" (445).

In chapter 32 with its pregnant beginning—"already we are boldly launched upon the deep; but soon we shall be lost in its unshored, harborless immensities" (116)—we plunge precipitently into the impenetrably factual world of cetology. But these cetological chapters will prove again and again to contain a sudden figurative sentence or two that plummets us to a deeper sounding. Some of these cohere in a particular set of associations—majesty, beauty, omniscience, ubiquity, and mystery. The "blanket" of the whale's skin is covered with undecipherable hieroglyphics; his separated eyes indicate a brain "so much more comprehensive, combining, and subtle than man's" (280; ch. 74) that can unite opposite views; observing his forehead "you feel the Deity and the dread powers more forcibly than in beholding any other object in living nature" (292; ch. 79); his brain conveys "the truest though not the most exhilarating conception of what the most exalted potency is; (294; ch. 80); his spout is engendered by his "incommunicable contemplations" (314; ch. 85); and his tail is like God's "back parts" (318; ch. 86), which Moses was permitted to see, though God's face was hidden, as the whale, too, is faceless—and so on and on until the Jovian white bull whale has destroyed his pursuers, his questioners. Now, do such hints suggest that the whale is nothing but a symbol after all, that we should consider the cetological material but hugely piled symbolic extravagance?

Here the patient, sequential, chapter-by-chapter close reading alone can be helpful, I find. The prosaic must be felt to have the weight that its quantity and detail conveys, some places so great as to make the metaphorical impulse seem a trivial diversion. At other times the prosaic is altogether subdued to metaphor. There are the great set pieces of metaphysical wit, like "The Monkey-Rope," "The Mat-Maker," and, of course, "The Whiteness of the Whale." There are such thoroughly poetic set pieces as "The Lee Shore," "The Mast-Head," "The Symphony," "The Try-Works." But then, some chapters are almost entirely peculiar and living fact, like the description of "The Grand Armada," which, except for a single wonderful sentence ("amid the tornadoed Atlantic of my being," etc. [326]) is simply superb reporting on nature's unending phenomenal mystery.

No, let us not allegorize it all or reduce it all to simple realism sprigged here and there with philosophy. As readers we must feel ourselves tossed back and forth between the one or the other way of reading exactly as the current dictates. This is, in part at least, what the book may be about—the endless and doomed insistence of the mind that all things have meaning, the otherness of nature that in the end swallows up the questioner. The rhythm of the book is a representation of humanity's alternating doubt and conviction that its questions can be answered. "What is Ahab's object?" our students ask. "Vengeance on a dumb brute that simply smote thee from blindest instinct!" Starbuck calls it; but Ahab answers that he would strike through the pasteboard mask, the "unreasoning mask" from behind which "some still reasoning thing puts forth the mouldings of its features." It is this conviction of meaning in nature that makes Ahab the obsessed transcendentalist for whom "not the smallest atom stirs or lives in matter, but has its cunning duplicate in mind . . ." (144; ch. 36). "Does Melville condemn Ahab?" we may ask our students. Not altogether, I think, for the very method of the book shows that he shares Ahab's quest. He is "one of that crew" bent on compelling utterance from the serene and baffling silence. "Some certain significance lurks in all things, else all things are little worth and the round world itself but an empty cipher, except to sell by the cartload," Ishmael says in "The Doubloon" (358). Yet the chapter goes on to demonstrate that everyone reads a personal meaning into the symbols of the world. On the masthead, in a swooning reverie of immersion in the All, Ishmael must recover in time that knowledge which separates perceiving man from the sea of dissolving forms. Beneath his feet is only sharkish reality, which can have no communion with his dreaming spirit perched so high aloft. But there is no last word. The great shroud of the sea rolls on, and Ishmael lives, buoyed by his coffin on this annihilating salt sea.

An inspired inconclusiveness in Melville's only real conclusion, after all, and a certain inconclusiveness in teaching *Moby-Dick* seems to me proper. *Moby-Dick* is certainly one of those works of the past that embrace a calculated indeterminacy beyond even the indeterminacy that may be present in all texts. The discontinuities of style, the vacillation between thematic pointedness and objective presentation of the "real"—these features raise the degree of "reader participation," stimulate our own effort to construct and integrate while reminding us of the chaos of being in which our hopes must bury themselves. If the reader "writes" the text, as it is now fashionable to suggest, then the text that conspicuously shifts the burden of meaning onto our shoulders should be allowed its own undecidability—this is likely to be the only "message" it can be said to impart.

Nothing our students discover, frustrated yet fascinated, is more elusive than the message we may search for among the explicit philosophic portions of the text. *Moby-Dick*'s dramatic structure offers a staged debate, and even the narrative voice, as we had noted, is inconsistent—the Ishmael who cheerfully dismisses the whole question of religion with "hell is an idea first born on an undigested apple-dumpling" (82; ch. 17) is in a different mood from the skeptical yet profoundly serious speaker who says, "like wilful travellers in Lapland, who refuse to wear colored and coloring glasses upon their eyes so the wretched infidel gazes himself blind at the monumental white shroud that wraps all the prospect around him" (170; ch. 42). We have come to realize that the concept of the unreliable narrator may extend to include almost any narrator, that the voice that seems most vested with authority, most identifiable with the author, offers only a hypothesis to be tested. Melville's narrative voice, by its very variability—now seeming to belong to Ishmael, now choral or orphic—will itself offer a changing series of responses to its own tale.

It was Forster, in *Aspects of the Novel*, the famous little book to which I referred earlier, who called Melville a "prophetic" writer, explaining that "his theme is the universe or something universal, but he is not necessarily going to 'say' anything about the universe; he proposes to sing" (116). The world of *Moby-Dick*, Forster went on to say, "is not a veil, it is not an allegory. It is the ordinary world of fiction, but it reaches back" (124). To what? To a song without words, a tribute to mystery, which we transcribe into speech only to falsify. "*Moby-Dick* is full of meanings: its meaning is a different problem. It is wrong to turn the *Delight* or the coffin into symbols, because even if the symbolism is correct, it silences the book. Nothing can be stated about *Moby-Dick* except that it is a contest. The rest is song" (130). I like to end my class discussions of *Moby-Dick* with Forster's somewhat out-of-fashion words. Melville's masterpiece does not boil down in our try-pot, and if it states anything it is that experience is ultimately irreducible to thought—but it is itself reducible neither to this meaning nor to any other.

Moby-Dick as Tragedy and Comedy

William H. Shurr

Over several years of reading and teaching *Moby-Dick* I have developed the following method of presenting the book to undergraduate students. The method involves a consideration first of Ahab as a tragic figure and then of Ishmael as a comedic figure. These are surely not the only discernible structures in the book, but, pedagogically, they allow me to introduce the major elements of plot and symbolism in an interesting and orderly way.

In the first stage I approach Captain Ahab's pursuit of the whale as a tragic quest. Melville clearly portrays Ahab as a tragic hero—"a mighty pageant creature, formed for noble tragedies" (71; ch. 16)—and also presents his own theory of tragedy, an advance on Aristotle's, in "The Mat-Maker" (ch. 47). Aristotle proposes the dynamics of action, in tragedy at least, as follows: action flows from a combination of the agent's character (*ethos*), developed over a long period of time, and the immediate thought processes (*dianoia*) that are going on when the agent faces a choice (Greek text of the *Poetics*, 1449^{b}36–1450^{a}3). As Melville analyzes the causes of action, his characters seem to operate in a larger, less sharply rational and defined world of "chance, free will, and necessity—no wise incompatible—all interweavingly working together" (185; ch. 47).

The whale, as object of the tragic quest, evolves as simultaneously divine and demonic in Ahab's mind. He is the monster-god of American Calvinism, which I describe more fully in *Rappaccini's Children: American Writers in a Calvinistic World*. A key word, which I italicize for emphasis in the following passage, attaches to the whale an attribute that, in the entire history of the word, has been applied only to God: "all their enchanted eyes intent upon the whale, which from side to side strangely vibrating his *predestinating* head, sent a broad band of overspreading semicircular foam before him as he rushed" (468; ch. 135).

As tragic hero, like Prometheus, Ahab undertakes to slay this monster-god, both for his private revenge and for humankind. But the reader comes to see, through multiple clues attached to Ahab, that this highly mythologized involvement with the demon-divine is both madness and blasphemy (madness on pp. 144, 160–61, 459 [chs. 36, 41, 134], etc.; blasphemy on pp. 87, 144, 147, 417, 459 [chs. 19, 36, 37, 119, 134], etc.). Ahab's quest and fall have many similarities with those of the protagonists of the classic tragedies. The careful reader is surely involved in the "pity and terror" that Aristotle suggests as the appropriate response to tragic action.

In a second stage I take a clue from Henry James, on point of view, that the most interesting element of the story may lie not in the tale but in the teller, the center of consciousness within the story. Thus I focus on Ishmael, who begins the tale in a sensitive and vulnerable mood (suicidal, on p. 12

[ch. 1]); he is off balance and ripe for experiences that will change and enlighten him.

Initially, Ishmael is swept totally into the magnetic orbit of Ahab's mad supernaturalistic monomania; chapter 41 begins,

> I, Ishmael, was one of that crew; my shouts had gone up with the rest; my oath had been welded with theirs; and stronger I shouted, and more did I hammer and clinch my oath, because of the dread in my soul. A wild, mystical, sympathetical feeling was in me; Ahab's quench-less feud seemed mine. (155)

But with the first sentence of chapter 42 a crucial transition begins: "What the white whale was to Ahab, has been hinted; what, at times, he was to me, as yet remains unsaid" (163).

Ishmael becomes more meditative, at once more realistic and more phil-osophical. He pulls away from Ahab in two ways: he investigates, in a more rationalistic way, both the lore and the science of the whale (in the cetological chapters), studying and reducing the mythologized materials that had ac-cumulated around it; and he begins to find sources of health and wholeness within himself. This last development comes to a climax in chapter 87, "The Grand Armada," where Ishmael finds the peaceful center of the whale herd to be an analogue for the deep center of peace that he has discovered within himself: "But even so, amid the tornadoed Atlantic of my being, do I myself still for ever centrally disport in mute calm; . . . there I still bathe me in eternal mildness of joy" (326). This experience is not a religious conversion. Ishmael in fact parodies such conversion with an exuberant and robust vision of his own, the comic masturbatory vision of angels in chapter 94, "A Squeeze of the Hand." If Ahab moves along a tragic line through his story, Ishmael's development is surely through the comedic and on into the satiric and ironic.

Ishmael becomes the first fully liberated and secularized hero of our lit-erature ("And *I only* am escaped *alone* to tell thee" [470; Epilogue]), the first to liberate himself in a conscious and methodological way. This is part of the reason why *Moby-Dick* is an important American book. He also escapes with a message ("And I only am escaped alone *to tell thee*"), and thus he engages even modern readers as our own Ancient Mariner. (In the "Spring"chapter of *Walden*, Thoreau had also led his readers through a series of meditations and exercises, to arrive at the visionary experience of "the Artist who made the world and me," and Melville once again counters the Transcendentalists.)

Other aspects of *Moby-Dick* can be considered, as subsidiary systems that feed into and amplify these two major lines, in a third stage of classroom discussion: Starbuck and Father Mapple, with their simple and sincere orthodoxies, probably represent the ordinary general reader's position among Melville's supposed original audience; the inverted baptism and eucharist ceremonies (in chs. 36 and 113) illuminate both the demonic nature of Ahab's quest and the strength of his hold on the crew: "The Doubloon" (ch. 99) reminds the reader that there are many ways to view a whale or a whaling tale; Pip's madness confirms that the universe contains terrors fearful enough to justify Ahab's crazy self-destructive response to them; Queequeg's simple humanistic paganism sets Ishmael further off balance at the beginning of the book, moving him to consider human loyalties as perhaps prior to and more satisfying than his "infallible Presbyterian" orthodoxies (54; ch. 10); and the "gams" with the other ships display alternative ways of coping with the whale and detecting his significance.

I assume, in presenting this reading, that the student is approaching *Moby-Dick* for the first time. If the presentation seems overly structured, it is because the beginning student needs some sense of success or accomplishment in comprehending this complex masterpiece. The guide will point out darker corridors for later exploration but will attempt to give at least a workable sense of the whole to the novice tourist. The reading outlined above offers a certain aesthetic satisfaction, a sense of the whole that provides the student with some control over a major work of art, and a sense that there are still further dimensions to investigate.

Moby-Dick: The Rationale of Narrative Form

Robert Milder

When I teach *Moby-Dick* in the Norton Critical Edition I like to assign my students Walter E. Bezanson's "*Moby-Dick*: Work of Art," which remains one of the best essays on Melville's book ever written. If it is a class of graduate students I am teaching, or a group of undergraduates studying Melville in depth, I may frame the assignment by telling them that Bezanson's essay marks a turning point in Melville criticism in two important respects: its presentation of Ishmael, not Ahab, as "the real center of meaning and the defining force of the novel," and its understanding of *Moby-Dick* as a book continuously in process. "Ishmael's vast symbolic prose poem in a free organic form," Bezanson calls the book, merging the two themes in a way that would set the tone for more than a quarter century of criticism (655,671).

I admire Bezanson's essay enormously, but I find its account of form the kind of question begging that Northrop Frye had in mind when he compared interpreters of *Moby-Dick* to "the doctors of Brobdingnag, who after great wrangling finally pronounced Gulliver a *lusus naturae*" (*Anatomy* 313). *Moby-Dick* is not a novel, a romance, an epic, an anatomy, or a tragedy, but it does contain elements of all these genres, and the ways they function individually and combine to form a whole ought to tell us something about the book's informing design. If *Moby-Dick* is an "organic" book, why not try to discover the principle of its organicism?

There are strong reasons for not trying. Melville, we know, was not a planner; at the extreme he was not even a good organicist, for his willingness to yield to a new idea, even a new controlling intention, sometimes usurped his commitments of form in ways that Coleridge, organicism's theorist, never foresaw. This is what happened with *Mardi* but not, I think, with *Moby-Dick*, where at some point during the process of composition Melville reconceived his book in light of an impelling vision and proceeded to marshal his materials accordingly in the series of chapters beginning with "The Lee Shore" and culminating in "Moby-Dick" and "The Whiteness of the Whale" (see Milder, "Composition").

In teaching *Moby-Dick* I try to spend as much time as I can afford on these chapters. I show my students how Melville begins by reasserting the quest motif established in "Loomings" ("The Lee Shore"), then sets out to elevate his subject ("The Advocate" and "Postscript"), introduce his cast of characters (the two "Knights and Squires"), adumbrate his theme (the Anacharsis Clootz passage from the second "Knights and Squires"), and finally reveal his protagonist ("Ahab"), whom he goes on to characterize in a non-Ishmaelean dramatic chapter ("Enter Ahab; to him, Stubb") and a soliloquy ("The Pipe"). I also take up some of the more problematic aspects of Melville's presentation, often in response to student questions: Why does Melville emphasize Starbuck's spiritual weakness and impair the potentially dramatic conflict between captain and mate? Why does Melville depart from the perspective of Ishmael and present Ahab "objectively," as if he were on stage?

More and more these basic questions about authorial choice have struck me as the ones to ask, if not always in class then at least before class, for myself. And increasingly I have found that my answers make sense only if they cohere and become elements of a single answer. However thoroughly I may explicate *Moby-Dick*'s thematic whats and technical hows, the principle of unity I need to teach the book effectively seems to lie in some invisible life within and behind them, in an immanent why.

A tentative formulation of this principle of life is what I mean by a "rationale." The term is R. S. Crane's and calls to mind the rhetorical tradition of the Chicago critics (140–94), but one might as easily invoke the vocabulary of, say, Roland Barthes when he describes the "structuralist activity" as an effort "to reconstruct an 'object' in such a way as to manifest thereby [its] rules of functioning" (158). Whatever words we use, the principle we want must explain not only the relation of parts within the closed system of the text but the orchestration of effects through time. In its engagement of the reader in the topic and tone immediately at hand, *Moby-Dick* is as temporal a book as we will ever find; yet like a symphony, which is also temporal, *Moby-Dick* takes its audience through an experience that has a determinable shape, and the nature and kinetic pattern of this experience are at once the center of the book's meaning and the source of its irregular but not arbitrary form.

The rationale that guides my teaching of *Moby-Dick* is one I find persuasive myself, but other explanations may do as well or better, and none can ever account for the whole of Melville's book or aspire beyond the status of a more or less satisfying critical fiction. What I want most to suggest in this essay is not a particular content but a way of thinking about *Moby-Dick* that takes the book's organicism as a starting point for investigation. There are numberless places to begin, and in class I like to generate a reading of the book from close attention to chapters 23–42. Here I would go back a step or two to some preliminary questions about narrative form. How does Melville present his two major blocks of material, Ishmael's whaling voyage and Ahab's hunt for Moby Dick? How does his presentation shape our changing involvement with the characters and action? And what informing design or rhetorical end is this pattern of involvement inferably made to serve?

I

As early as the second sen·ence of *Moby-Dick* we know the book we will
be reading is a retrospective first-person narrative, but even the dullest
student soon realizes that it will be no ordinary novel or romance. Even in
"Loomings" Ishmael shows himself an excessively talky narrator by fictional
standards, and the hand he proffers us in the half-casual, half-peremptory
"Call me Ishmael" draws us through the frame of the narrative in a manner
that even long-time readers of *Moby-Dick* find disconcerting. "We are going
a-whaling," Ishmael tells us in the "The Carpet-Bag," taking us by the arm
and escorting us through the door of the Spouter-Inn, then dropping suddenly into the second person ("Entering that gable-ended Spouter-Inn, you
found . . . "), telling us what we would have seen, how we would have felt
(19–20).

"The writer's audience is always a fiction," Walter J. Ong has said; the
writer imagines "an audience cast in some sort of role" and by appropriate
signs tries to ensure that the audience will "correspondingly fictionalize
itself" (60–61). Ishmael's audience in "Loomings" is cast in the role of would-
be adventurers: respectable landsmen "tied to counters, nailed to benches,
clinched to desks" who secretly yearn for the sea and who realize (once
Ishmael shows them) that the object of their yearning is "the ungraspable
phantom of life" (12–13, 14). Ishmael is their (our) surrogate, who, having
gone to sea and returned, spirits us away with him as he retraces his course,
assuming (like so many of Whitman's narrators) the dual part of companion
and tutor. He is a tour guide carrying us over traveled ground, making his
past impressions our present ones and filling us, as we go, with his story;
but he is also a voice speaking in our ear, commenting, interpreting, explaining, besieging us writer-to-reader in the book's temporal "now" even
as he enlists our participation in the reenacted whaling voyage.

Why does Ishmael tell his story? To discover the meaning of his experience, we commonly hear; yet much of Ishmael's narration, particularly in
the cetological chapters, has little direct relation to his experience. Students
remark on this and are notoriously impatient with these long desert stretches
of information shot through with philosophy and whimsical humor that have
no precedent in their experience of the novel. Their response is hardly
surprising, for the passages they find tedious or puzzling belong to a different
tradition of fiction, in which a speculative interest predominates over storytelling and characters and events engage the writer primarily as subjects for
reflection or sources of imaginative play; the passages belong to the "extro-
verted and intellectual" tradition of the anatomy (Frye, *Anatomy* 308). Though
Moby-Dick is, or contains, a novelistic story of education, it encloses this

story within a larger "spoken" action whose reference is not inward to the motives and psychology of the narrator, as it ordinarily would be in a first-person novel, but outward to the extratextual world the narrator shares with us.

When I discuss Ishmael's story in class, I focus, as I imagine most teachers do, on the prominent moments of discovery along the way—those in "A Bosom Friend," "The Hyena," "The Monkey-Rope," "The Grand Armada," "A Squeeze of the Hand," and "The Try-Works," among others—but I am equally concerned with describing the consciousness that emerges from these chapters and informs Ishmael's present-tense commentary. The Ishmael who goes to sea in lieu of pistol and ball is a descendant of the morose young Redburn, toughened by experience but still quarreling with a society of professed Christians who behave like cannibals. The world of New Bedford and Nantucket, I show my students (as Robert Zoellner has shown me), is an ossified, flinty-hearted world evoked by images of winter and bleakness and biting frost and by the spiritual frost of Father Mapple's chastising Calvinist God and Bildad's counting-house heaven (see Zoellner, ch. 4). Before Ishmael can give himself freely to the spiritual adventure of going to sea, he needs to unburden himself of this husk of a world with its inca-pacitating psychic hold on him. He does this in "A Bosom Friend," and students are quick to note the irony of a misanthrope converted to Christian brotherhood by a cannibal and sealing his commitment by participating in a heathen rite. They are less apt to see that what Ishmael learns from Queequeg is not simply a new fraternity but a new ideal of being, a "calm self-collectedness of simplicity" (52; ch. 10) not unlike Emerson's "noncha-lance of boys who are sure of a dinner" ("Self-Reliance" 29) but more affec-tionate, sensuous, and playful.

To help characterize this consciousness I like to introduce two passages from outside the text: D. H. Lawrence's remark on *Typee* and *Omoo* that though "We can't go back to the savages: not a stride, . . . we can take a great curve in their direction, onwards," (137) and Melville's comment to Hawthorne that the men who say "NO! in thunder" are "in the happy condition of judicious, unincumbered travellers in Europe; they cross the frontiers into Eternity with nothing but a carpet-bag,—that is to say, the Ego" (Davis and Gilman 125). In wedding himself to Queequeg, Ishmael assimilates an ideal of Polynesian wholeness and serenity of being to his speculative Western consciousness and begins a journey that will lead him to the other side of civilization, beyond primitivism and New Bedford alike. He has sloughed off both society's systems, oughts, and musts and the rebel's compulsion to resist them, and he wanders through the universe a sovereign self "owning no allegiance but to the King of the Cannibals" (232; ch. 57) and resembling a metaphysical version of the picaro.

I find this last comparison helpful when I pass from Ishmael's conversion in "A Bosom Friend" to the confrontation of self and world that soon becomes the focus of his voyage of discovery. In "The Hyena," Ishmael's first encounter with the indifference of the sea, the alienation of the New Bedford chapters reemerges as an ontological condition and calls forth a sense of jaunty, uncompromised outlawry such as the picaro feels toward respectable society. I develop the analogy further when I discuss "The Monkey-Rope," in which Ishmael's humorously appalled discovery of an "interregnum in Providence" (271) extends the theme of cosmic indifference and evolves the ethical corollary that humans must provide the solicitude that former ages entrusted to God. Robert Alter has characterized the picaresque hero as at once "an image of human solitude in the world" and "an image of human solidarity in the world" (10). So, in a more visibly existential way, Ishmael, whose humanitarianism emerges from a backdrop of universal emptiness. Pip, alone on the ocean, is Melville's image for the human condition at its starkest and truest, and it seems no accident of positioning that "The Castaway" is followed by the most fraternal of *Moby-Dick*'s chapters, "A Squeeze of the Hand." The Ishmael who bobs up clinging to Queequeg's coffin is still a wanderer and an outcast, but his name has come to signify a cosmic, not a social, exile. Like all of us, he is the world's orphan.

In assembling these scenes in which Ishmael steps forward as an actor, I am always surprised at how few of them there are. A half dozen chapters, or fewer than thirty pages out of 470, are enough to suggest the main lines of Ishmael's development. Altogether, Melville seems less interested in the novelistic possibilities of character change than in what Ishmael's achieved vision allows him to see and in how the vehicle of retrospective narrative can lend itself to refracted authorial commentary.

For most students, discursiveness in fiction is as appealing as eight o'clock classes, and learning to read Melville with pleasure requires suspending much of what they have been previously taught about the novel. The chronology of the syllabus is an advantage here, for undergraduates in a survey course who come to Melville from Emerson and Thoreau will already have discovered the speculative nature of mid-nineteenth-century American literature and are prepared to find *Moby-Dick* less anomalous than it might seem to a class studying the art of fiction. I stress the impulse toward exploration Melville shared with Emerson, Thoreau, and Whitman; but in graduate courses I also like to account for Melville's practice in *Moby-Dick* by noting its generic origin in his semi- or quasi-autobiographical travel narratives, its debt to nonnovelistic traditions of intellectual and satiric prose, and its status as a compromise between his inclinations and his purse. After experimenting disastrously with an allegorical romance (*Mardi*) and halfheartedly with a novel of initiation whose point of view he could not sustain (*Redburn*), Melville discovered a congenial narrative form in *White-Jacket*. To accommodate his bent for "talk" and yet satisfy an audience that demanded a fictional plot, he enclosed a rudimentary narrative of education involving the jacket within a microcosmic anatomy of "our man-of-war world"—the sailor White-Jacket evolving toward the perspective of the present-tense narrator, who surveyed experience through eyes that were fundamentally Melville's without sacrificing his autonomy as a fictional character. What *White-Jacket* did with life in the navy *Moby-Dick* does with the enterprise of whaling, with three important differences: the character-narrator has considerably more savor; his narrated action is elevated into a metaphysical quest; and his present-tense anatomy is broadened from the relation of classes in Western society (*White-Jacket*'s allegorical subject) to humanity's position in the universe at large.

Teaching the anatomy is more difficult than teaching the narrative, partly because Ishmael's reflections are scattered throughout the text and partly because students are prone to simplify his many-layered ironies toward himself, his subject, life in general, and the gullible or straight-faced reader (never ourselves, of course). A short assignment on one of the expository chapters can help illustrate how Ishmael transforms whaling fact into philosophical speculation or imaginative play, but the real challenge is to suggest, in a day's class, the cumulative significance of the whole. Just as Samuel Johnson felt that "a system of civil and economical prudence" might be drawn from Shakespeare's works, so might a social and metaphysical "system" be drawn from *Moby-Dick*; for casual and mood-dependent as they are, Ishmael's reflections do cohere in a philosophy of life—skeptical, unillusioned, absurdist, humanitarian. Almost invariably, however, Ishmael's reflections turn back on themselves, mocking their own moralism with a double-edged metaphor or an obscene pun, at once constructing and deconstructing the truth of the moment because (Ishmael knows) there is always something more, and something other, to be said. Finally, then, what one wants to communicate in class is not a set of conclusions but an activity of mind that proceeds from the "deep inland" certainty of self Ishmael describes in "The Grand Armada" (326) and that is content to take the universe by pieces, squeezing each discrete fact for what it will yield to the imagination and presenting an example of redeemed consciousness working on the world.

When I think about the overall form of Ishmael's narrative—a past-tense journey of discovery contained within a present-tense anatomy—the analogies that come to mind are not to any works of fiction but to *Walden* and "Song of Myself," works predicated on a promise of knowledge in which the hero ventures out into the world, explores it as a metaphysical scout, and returns to the settlements to report his findings in a literary form at once narrative and instructional. The hero is initially an outsider from the community (though like Whitman's narrator he may pretend not to be), but through the rhetoric of the work he implicates the reader in its rehearsed action, educates or awakens him by means of his sustained commentary, and shapes a new cultural order around what he and his audience have learned. Though Ishmael the narrator has been formed by his voyage aboard the *Pequod*, his present-tense discursiveness is not simply or primarily a psychological coda to a story of education; it is an action in its own right, which illuminates and extends the body of experience we have been acquiring. Thus the concertedly "oral" basis of Ishmael's narration—the direct addresses to the reader, the mock dialogues and rhetorical questions, the banter, the exhortations, all of which (so prophetic of Thoreau's and Whitman's) are common enough in "thematic" genres like the anatomy but well outside the mainstream of the novel or romance (Frye, *Anatomy* 52). Unlike *The Scarlet Letter* or *The Ambassadors*, *Moby-Dick*, I show my students, is not a book that aspires to *be*, as New Critics liked to describe the urnlike status of novels and poems, or even to mean. It is a work whose narrative form indicates a governing intention to *do* something to us as we read, to remake us.

II

The difference between *Moby-Dick*, on one hand, and *Walden* and "Song of Myself," on the other, is that Melville's narrator is also engaged in telling the story of someone else. As early as chapter 16 when Ahab is first described by Peleg and Ishmael is seized with "a strange awe of him" (77), *Moby-Dick* departs from Melville's earlier books and ranges itself with a class of fictions variously characterized as "meditations on the hero," "observer-hero narratives," and "interpreted designs," works in which the story of the hero is filtered through the consciousness of a first-person narrator and assimilated to the broader story of the narrator's own life (see Reed; Buell; Minter). The category is a useful one that links *Moby-Dick* with at least two other books I commonly teach in an undergraduate survey, *The Great Gatsby* and *Absalom, Absalom!*, but it does not tell me what I most need to know: why Melville chose not to abide by the limitations of his point of view but instead gave us soliloquies that Ishmael could not have overheard (if indeed they were spoken at all), conversations at which none but the participants were present, chapters cast in dramatic and quasi-dramatic form, and a long narrative conclusion in which Ishmael disappears entirely and is replaced by an omniscient third-person voice.

Students schooled in the novel and encountering *Moby-Dick* for the first time often raise this question when they reach the stage directions that title chapter 29 ("Enter Ahab; to Him, Stubb"), the soliloquy in chapter 30 ("The Pipe"), and the omniscient point of view in chapter 31 ("Queen Mab"); they had been prepared for a first-person narrative and are puzzled by Melville's dereliction. I introduce the common explanation—that Ishmael, hampered by the incompleteness of his knowledge and the constraints of conventional storytelling, invents these scenes to render the imaginative truth of his voyage aboard the *Peqoud*—and am generally greeted by skepticism. It is not the ingenuity of the argument that disturbs students so much as their feeling that, plausible or not, this reading has nothing to do with their experience of the chapters.

The real issue here is not whether Ishmael or Melville is the "author" of *Moby-Dick* but whether the author, whoever he is, appears in these sections as what Bezanson calls "the enfolding sensibility, . . . the imagination through which all matters of the book pass" (655). Do these chapters have the authority of third-person omniscience or the self-reference of even the most "reliable" first-person narration?

There are thirteen dramatic chapters in *Moby-Dick* (29, 36–40, 108, 119–22, 127, 129), if we count only those that use stage directions, more if we include chapters in which an opening narrative passage introduces a soliloquy, a series of parallel soliloquies, or a play of voices that imitates the exchanges of characters on stage (see also Barbour 177–78). The common factor in all is the absence of any observable perspective—visual, moral, or psychological—on the action. In chapters like "Sunset," "The Quarter-Deck," or "The Candles," Melville's form bridges the distance that fiction establishes between character and reader, and it places us as directly in Ahab's presence as the conventions of printed literature will allow. We are exposed to Ahab's spell much as Ishmael had been, but it is not out of faithfulness to Ishmael's experience that Melville constructs the chapters as he does. Even in scenic narration it is possible to retain a semblance of the character-narrator's point of view without sacrificing dramatic immediacy by interposing an actual voice; all the author need do is locate a "point of observation" somewhere within the scene itself, so that we have "the illusion of being present . . . in one of [its] figures" (Stanzel 23). In *Moby-Dick*, however, we witness the dramatic scenes from outside and credit them with an objectivity that normally belongs only to the drama. Ishmael is nowhere in sight or in mind, and it does not occur to us, as we are reading the chapters, that they are his "inventions." Our attention is focused wholly on Ahab, whose size increases with proximity and whose power we are left to confront as best we can without the moral guardianship of the narrator.

Students who come to *Moby-Dick* by way of "Hawthorne and His Mosses," as mine do, often account for the dramatic chapters by citing the influence of Shakespeare, who they know was on Melville's mind in 1850–51 and whose presence in *Moby-Dick* they find palpable. I acknowledge their point but ask them to consider what dramatic techniques do in *Moby-*

Dick—specifically, how they affect our relation to Ahab's hunt.

The hunt itself, I will have suggested in class, is a reenactment of the "dragon-killing theme" that Frye describes as the "central form of quest romance" (*Anatomy* 189), a theme Melville signals by his fifth extract (Isaiah's prophecy of the slaying of Leviathan [2]) and by Ishmael's reference to Moby Dick as a "Job's whale" (162; ch. 41). In marshaling the human race for a grand climactic assault on the biblical "sea-monster . . . associated with chaos" (*Oxford Annotated Bible* 653), Ahab is thus something more, or other, than tragedy's "great man"; he is the scapegoat-hero who plays out humanity's common fantasy of slaying the dragon, or father, or tyrannical god who has dispossessed him of the paradisiacal life he feels is rightfully his.

An action like this is of a different mimetic order from the actions of Shakespearean tragedy or from anything students are likely to have met in the novel. It is what Henry A. Murray has called "a mythic event" or an essentially symbolic occurrence "represented in sensory terms," which enlists the reader's imagination because it appeals to "emotions, wants, and actions" that "are present as potential tendencies in virtually all men and women of all societies and times" ("Definitions" 8, 16). Novels may have mythic elements, too, but these usually take the form of archetypal patterns enacted by the characters with reference to their fictional world, not rituals that involve the audience in a symbolic action. This latter, communal function of myth has traditionally been served by the drama, whose qualities of immediacy, objectivity, elevation, and artifice are most effective in commanding the absorbed yet distanced participation that myth-as-ritual requires.

As a matter of simple decorum, Ahab's hunt demanded the elevation of a high mimetic mode like dramatic tragedy in which the heroes' power of action is greater than our own, their language more sublime, and their world more amenable to hints of the divine (Frye, *Anatomy* 34–35, 50). But the form of Ahab's action is functional in another way, for the heightening techniques that contribute so largely to our involvement with the hunt—the unmediated, "theatrical" presentation; the dense and sometimes cryptic allusions; the labored "poetic" prose; above all, the Shakespearean coloring—are continuous reminders that we are in a literary rather than a real world. Reading "The Candles," we never think to ask whether Ahab was actually struck by lightning (as readers of *The Marble Faun* asked about Donatello's furry ears), nor are we troubled that the fiery spirit Ahab addresses seems to answer him, as the gods in our world would not. The artifice of the chapter exempts it from comparison to reality and invites us to give Ahab's defiance what I. A. Richards called "emotional belief," or a belief that arises from and fulfills a psychic need without soliciting intellectual or moral assent or requiring us to act on its consequences (255–74). The feeling of holiday that artifice can create is important for any mythic action that has no analogue in the real world; for a blasphemous action like Ahab's that taps hidden resentments and threatens to burden us with unacceptable guilt, it may be the essential condition for participation.[1]

For the landsman reader, drawn into "Moby Dick" by Ishmael's brooding intensity and made a party to his cosmic terror by the technique of "The Whiteness of the Whale," angers and frustrations that had been repressed are raised to consciousness, then licensed by Ishmael's own "wild, mystical, sympathetical feeling" (155; ch. 41) toward the hunt and mobilized in a vicarious revenge that promises all the gratification of a sudden unloosing of buried impulse and all the safety of fantasy and daydream. But the reader's sense of safety is illusory. The genteel landsman's self has been betrayed by the rhetorically induced welling up of a universal but culturally forbidden sense of experience. The reader has been "unmade."

Ishmael keys our response to the hunt in chapters 41 and 42 when by making "Ahab's quenchless feud" his own and the crew's (155), he makes it seem the reader's. Since students resist being told how they feel or ought to feel, I like to present these chapters as they might have struck an imagined reader of 1851, the typical "landsman" implied by the rhetoric of "Loomings." This reader is educated, genteel, and conventionally religious—"not true, or undeveloped," to quote "The Try-Works" (355), but a better word might be "repressed," for the reader's baggage of orthodoxy requires a denial not merely of a whole class of thoughts and perceptions but of an inescapable human anger at the order of things.

By going to sea with Ishmael the landsman leaves behind the prejudices of the shore world and ventures out expectantly, secure in Ishmael's tutelage. The introduction of Ahab—first obscurely in "The Ship" and the Elijah chapters, later in full—reveals a different and unanticipated kind of book, one the reader might never have begun at all had it shown its colors at the outset. Not until "Moby Dick" and "The Whiteness of the Whale" is the reader brought, through Ishmael's mediation, to recognize a latent sympathy with the hunt. To the Ishmael of "Moby Dick" Ahab is "crazy Ahab" (160), his hatred of Creation morbid, his monomania insane. Yet having dissociated himself from Ahab's malevolent world and offered in its place a universe of whiteness, empty and annihilating, Ishmael is driven by the horror of his vision to an emotional endorsement of the quest. "Wonder ye then at the fiery hunt?" he concludes "The Whiteness of the Whale" (170), as if the appalling ice of nothingness justified one's going mad and joining with Ahab in hallucinating a fiery, personified world one might set out to defy.

A work that evokes feelings as primal as humanity's bitterness and resentment at the world it inhabits has an enormous power for conversion, for fastening its loose fish of a reader to whatever vision or belief the rhetoric of the book artfully provides. Countless unwritten *Moby-Dick*s lie hidden here, and in teaching the balance of the book I try to show how the wild hope and foreboding it arouses (*Moby-Dick*'s equivalent to tragedy's pity and fear) are directed by Melville toward a persuasional end. By this point I will have spent four days on *Moby-Dick*, all on chapters 1–46. After two days on the assorted material of chapters 47–105 and the world they bring forth, I reserve my final two days for a second look at Ahab and Ishmael.

I begin with Ahab's "intellectual and spiritual exasperations" (160; ch. 41), taking up the soliloquies and staged encounters in which Ahab comes forward and speaks his mind. I point out that unlike Shakespeare's tragic heroes, who are continuously in motion, Ahab is fixed, static, and immune to the pull of other characters, who are at most dramatic foils like Starbuck and the carpenter or symbolic accessories like Fedallah. I stress, however, that while Ahab remains constant (except to grow more furious as he nears Moby Dick), the allusions through which Melville shapes our response to him change considerably. In the early chapters Ahab was likened to heroes and redeemers—Perseus, Prometheus, Christ; now, in his obessiveness and "fatal pride" (425; ch. 124), the would-be savior is recast as a source of tyranny and inhumaneness who must himself be purged for the well-being of society.

Although the reader, like Ishmael, has identified with Ahab's hunt, not with Ahab, Melville's diabolization of Ahab has the rhetorical effect of *ad hominem* argument, which discredits a cause by vilifying its proponent. The man who began as the reader's surrogate does not become a simple villain or hero-villain but a scapegoat, or what Kenneth Burke called "a 'suppurating' device" (40), who absorbs the reader's cosmic anger and who is repudiated, expelled from the moral community of the audience, and finally slain, though not without performing the act of symbolic defiance the reader delegated him to perform. When Ahab thrusts the harpoon into Moby Dick—"*Thus, I give up the spear!*" (468; ch. 135)—the reader is at once with him and apart from him. The reader shares emotionally in the act of god-defiance, then acquiesces in the death of Ahab, the offending deicide in him- or herself.

The catharsis *Moby-Dick* effects is not a factitious one confined to a temporary identification with an imaginary character in an imaginary situation; it is, or aims to be, a purgation of impulses in the reader that antecede the book. What dies with Ahab, however, is not simply a morbid, defiant element within the reader's psyche but a cultural order and a mode of consciousness. The Ahab who is associated with Prometheus, Job, Christ, Satan, Macbeth, Lear, Faust, Manfred, and Cain, among others, is the legitimate heir of these literary and mythic figures; he sails toward his encounter with Moby Dick bearing the entire legacy of Western thought with its monotheism, its preoccupation with the problem of evil, and its hope for redemption from a fallen world through the mediation of a savior. In his energy and magnitude

Ahab is a throwback to Renaissance drama, but the problems that afflict him are those of the mid-century Victorian (the contemporary reader) who inherits a system of belief that can no longer answer or evade the questions put to it but whose tyranny over the terms of thought is nonetheless complete. Ahab is the last and fullest flowering of the Christian tradition, which now, in its death rattle, turns against itself and in the name of Christian values calls God to account for not behaving like God and destroys itself in a maddened act of immolation.

"The work of the hero," Joseph Campbell has said, "is to slay the tenacious aspect of the father (dragon, tester, ogre, king) and release from its ban the vital energies that feed the universe" ("Transformations" 122). In *Moby-Dick*, I like to suggest, there are two fathers, only one of whom can be slain. Just as Moby Dick (the dragon) is a creation symbol who like Job's Leviathan rules as "a king over all the children of pride" (41.34), so Ahab, king of the microcosmic *Pequod*, represents a way of conceiving and responding to Creation that has ruled the Western world at least since the Renaissance and has stamped its repressed, theocentric consciousness on the institutions of social and political life. The climactic confrontation of father with father resembles another cultural Armageddon I like to introduce in class, Carlyle's account of the Norse Twilight of the Gods, in which "the divine Powers [or heroes] and the chaotic brute ones . . . meet at last in [a] universal world-embracing wrestle and duel" that is "mutually extinctive; and ruin, 'twilight' sinking into darkness, swallows the created Universe" (275).[2] In *Moby-Dick's* duel the whale swims away, invincible; but insofar as the "universe" is an ordering and naming of experience that we bring into being by our categories of thought, it too perishes with Ahab. The work of the hero is accomplished in *Moby-Dick* by the hero's own sacrificial death.

III

The sea that closes round the vortex of the sinking *Pequod* engulfs the world as completely as darkness does in the Norse myth, but here also the death of the old order "is not a final death" (Carlyle 275). Up pops Ishmael clinging to Queequeg's coffin-lifebuoy, the lone survivor of this cultural Armageddon and (like the biblical Ishmael) the founder, or prototype, of a new race.

This is not an easy theme to teach. By the time they finish the chase scenes, students are exhausted by *Moby-Dick* and are already looking ahead to next week's reading. The book seems tragic to them, as it would be if the forlornness of Ishmael adrift on the ocean were not subsumed by playfulness and curiosity of Ishmael the narrator. In tragedy the group of chastened onlookers who gather round the body of the hero offer only the barest promise of a new order, but in *Moby-Dick* the downward curve of tragedy toward isolation and death is enclosed within an upward curve of comedy toward social renewal.

To emphasize this principle of enclosure I spend my final day of class on Ishmael. I will already have dealt with the cetological chapters and shown how, fact by fact, fancy by fancy, Ishmael brings before us an entire phenomenological "world" against whose backdrop, and within whose moral perimeter, Ahab is implicitly presented for judgment. Now I turn to Ishmael himself and rehearse the main lines of his development from "The Hyena" through the climactic structural unit that begins with "The Castaway" and ends with the closing three paragraphs of "The Try-Works." As far as possible I compare Ishmael's discoveries during the voyage with Ahab's "intellectual and spiritual exasperations," counterpointing specific chapters and suggesting how Ishmael's vision recognizes the same experiential facts that torment Ahab yet manages to return from "the congregation of the dead" (355; ch. 96).

I discuss these chapters at the last rather than as they occur because I have found that students cannot begin to "see" Ishmael until they have finished *Moby-Dick*. Ishmael himself is free to profit from the lessons of the voyage only because Ahab enacts for him, and cathartically expels, the Ahabian element within his own nature. In this respect, as in so many others, Ishmael's experience is a representation in the book of what the reader is made to feel through the disposition of materials and effects we call structure. Emptied and cut adrift by Ahab's death, the reader casts about for a moral lifeline and discovers Ishmael, who seems more remarkable the closer one looks at him. The epilogue itself is hardly an affirmation—dramatically, tonally, how could it be?—but it is enough to point the reader back to Ishmael and to the chronological conclusion of his experience, the writing of the tale, which is also the thematic conclusion of *Moby-Dick*. "Loomings," with its comic, absurdist vision of the "universal thump" (15), is the delayed sequel to the epilogue and the philosophical goal of Ishmael's journey as much as it is the narrative beginning. And gradually, in retrospect, as the reader retraces the imaginative journey and asks where it has led, he or she finds that its destination is not Ahab thrusting the harpoon into Moby Dick or Ishmael alone on the ocean but a buoyant, ludic voice, radically new, speaking of heaven and earth and offering not a message or a philosophy but an example of being. Part of the appeal of this example is Ishmael's frank recognition that the lessons of the voyage will have to be renewed. Nonetheless, the tone of the speaker in his ever-present now is exuberantly comic. When the hypos return, as they will, Ishmael will "quietly take to the ship" and purge them once more. And the reader, in his or her hypos, will take once more to *Moby-Dick*.

IV

On virtually every level—chronological, narrative, generic, ethical, and meta-physical—*Moby-Dick* works to enclose Ahab by Ishmael without wholly assimilating him to Ishmael. This enclosure is a principle of structure that tells us how *Moby-Dick* is put together; it becomes a rationale when, by examining the pattern of our responses, we understand the achieved form of the book as an attempt to expose the reader to the full and unmediated power of Ahab and then to encircle it, exorcise it. Melville, in this view, is not testing alternative visions of the world (Ahab's is never an intellectual possibility); he is involving his audience in a symbolic action designed to purge an old consciousness and bring forth a new one.

A rationale as "persuasional" as this inevitably asks that we look beyond the literary work to the cultural and biographical circumstances of the author. Within the context of the American Renaissance, *Moby-Dick* aligns itself with Emerson's lectures and addresses of the mid-to-late 1830s, with the earliest editions of *Leaves of Grass*, and with *Walden*, all of which set out to redeem the national experiment by fashioning the New World character long anticipated but still by 1835, then by midcentury, nowhere in sight—in Whitman's words, "to help the forming of a great aggregate Nation . . . through the forming of myriads of fully develop'd and enclosing individuals" (571). Whitman described his own project as "The Great Construction of the New Bible" (Bucke 57); what he meant was the kind of communal scripture, at once fictive and philosophical, that Northrop Frye has called an epic: "a narrative poem of heroic action, but a special kind of narrative" that "has an encyclopaedic quality to it, distilling the essence of all the religious, philosophical, political, even scientific learning of its time, and, if completely successful, the definitive poem for its age" (*Return* 5).[3] "The Epos is not yet sung," Emerson complained in 1838: "That is the gospel of glad tidings kings & prophets wait for" (Sealts, *Journals* 476). By 1860, the "Epos" had been sung three times: by Whitman in *Leaves of Grass*, Thoreau in *Walden*, and Melville in *Moby-Dick*.

Why each of the writers should have given himself to the problem of America is ultimately a psychological question that involves the general situation of the writer in America and the private impulses and conflicts behind each writer's work. America was the idiom in which Melville, Whitman, and Thoreau spoke, but it was never the cause or final substance of their speaking. In Melville's case, the need to order Ahabian and Ishmaelean elements within himself went back at least as far as *Mardi* and would remain a lifelong problem. More immediately, *Moby-Dick* belongs to an intellectual and emotional gestalt bounded on one side by "Hawthorne and His Mosses" and on the other by Melville's letters to Hawthorne from the autumn of

1851 and by the beginnings of *Pierre*. The relation of democracy and tragedy, Edenicism and Calvinism, Emerson and Hawthorne, preoccupied Melville during these months as a matter both of personal vision and of the author's public role in the American world. *Moby-Dick* was a temporary answer to these antinomies in which Melville the writer-prophet sought to refound fraternal democracy on a perception of the tragic while expelling the paralyzing and destructive anger that came from dwelling on the tragic in outworn terms of thought. "I have written a wicked book, and feel spotless as the lamb," Melville told Hawthorne in November 1851 (Davis and Gilman 142), revealing how fully he himself had vicariously plunged the harpoon into Moby Dick and, for the moment at least, been purged by it. All these considerations are a long way from our "rationale of narrative form," but questions of cultural and biographical context almost always arise in class, as they should, and any interpretation that concerns itself with authorial meaning must be able to deal with them. A rationale is a principle of formal analysis, but there is no end to the concentric circles of inquiry it can generate.

NOTES

[1]This is similar to psychological interpretations of literary form as a defensive mechanism. See Lesser, chs. 7 and 10, and Holland, chs. 3–4.

[2]Melville borrowed an edition of Carlyle's *On Heroes, Hero-Worship, and the Heroic in History* from Evert Duyckinck in June or July 1850 and seems to have had the Norse Twilight of the Gods in mind as he wrote the final scenes of *Moby-Dick*.

[3]Frye's definition of epic paraphrases that of the Renaissance critics, but it serves well both as a general definition of the epic's intent and as a description of how Melville, Thoreau, and Whitman liked to conceive their own work.

THE CLASSROOM SITUATION
Students and Teachers, Strategies and Structures

Moby-Dick as the Preservation of Reading

Bainard Cowan

Two points seem to me crucial to any reader's understanding of *Moby-Dick* and hence to any classroom consideration of the text. The first is the transformative nature of Ishmael's experience as both protagonist and narrator (and writer, too, although not author—all of these terms need reconsideration after a reading of *Moby-Dick*). Ishmael's progress is marked by several definite stages through which the narrative passes, each dominated by strikingly different attitudes and signifying relations. But since this question involves in part a strategic stance in a familiar old quarrel about reading *Moby-Dick*, I want to leave further discussion of it until I have taken up the second point, which to me is more pressing because more often neglected.

I am speaking of the intertextuality of *Moby-Dick*, an aspect central to the drama of its action and the production of its narrative. John Carlos Rowe writes of this newly current term that " 'intertextuality' does not indicate merely the strategy of reading one text with another, but the fact that every text is itself already an intertextual event" (qtd. in Lentricchia 175). In *Moby-Dick* this event has importance beyond mere theory. It constitutes Ishmael's—and through him Melville's—struggle with the whole of Western tradition, his search for a language that will both make sense—hence harmonizing with and repeating the voices of tradition—and critically assert his freedom from the death implicit in those vanished texts.

Such interaction is especially intense with the Bible, which has come down to Melville's and Ishmael's time as a text that in three senses "is not itself" (to quote Rowe again on intertextuality): (1) The Bible stands for the Western religious tradition—events of what is called "sacred history" as well as the belief in their past and continued efficacy. (2) As the King James Version, it stands for the fountainhead of poetic power in the English language. (3) As the privileged text associated with the Puritan founding of America and the development of New England industry, it stands for an authorization of Western and capitalist strategies of domination. Melville's "quarrel with God" is more precisely a quarrel with the last of these significations, that is, with a reading that justifies domination and views history as a series of conquests. Melville repeatedly and confidently insists in *Moby-Dick* that this reading of Scripture as the conqueror's proclamation is wrong. His quarrel is not a rejection of the Bible per se, clearly, since he announces his central strategy for subverting that triumphalist interpretation in the first sentence of his narrative—"Call me Ishmael." He searches the Bible, most often the Old Testament, for figures who personify loss, rejection, suffering, and expulsion from the conquering line—figures such as Ishmael, Rachel, and Lazarus—and finds in them the living reality of the biblical principles of faith.

Melville's strategy is in short to unseat a culturally confirmed reading of a foundation text but to do so in order to affirm its received message as a spiritual truth preserved within the heart, not within the institutions it has founded. The same dialectic of subversion and affirmation, neither position a final one, ties *Moby-Dick* to other foundational works—although somewhat less intimately than to the Bible—so that a confirmed intertextual dialogue prevails between it and *The Odyssey, The Aeneid*, and *The Divine Comedy*. All bear the general form of a hero's quest through foreign, dangerous waters or spheres for a redeemed destiny—a life set to order and given by the gods. Odysseus, however, confidently reaches home and wife and reestablishes order in the palace (see Horkheimer and Adorno, who view Odysseus as a bourgeois man, achieving his ends by a progressive domination and deprivation of his crew [43–78]), Aeneas is granted kingship and the new fruits of Italy, and Dante is permitted to glimpse the final union of God with humanity at the end of his heavenly journey. Ishmael has no palace, no kingship, no wife, no native land; and his vision of unity—the whales' breeding ground, a natural harmony excluding human beings—is followed, not prefaced, by his narrow escape from a destructive vortex.

This multiple negation of homecoming and unification suggests several critical theses: that the westering movement of founding and expansion has come to an end; that the enterprise of Protestant bourgeois capitalism has in principle gone bankrupt; that being, as Heidegger might say, after having been enthroned for too long in the West at the expense of coming into and out of being, now must be displaced by a more Heraclitean consciousness; or that, as Derrida might contend, a letter does not always reach its destination, the signifier does not inevitably find its signified, and the real action of signification, hence of reading, hence of understanding, is to follow the trace of the signifier—a process of endless dissemination.

But the chief thing about this intertextual dialectic in *Moby-Dick* is that it does happen. It is not merely an intellectual framework. *Moby-Dick* is vitally involved with the major texts of the West and sets up an interplay with them instead of superseding them. Its position is not an "American Adam"–style forgetting of classical and European works but an intimate relation with them that begins by opposing their foundational function, what some would call their mythological element (in that they constrain rather than liberate our thinking about human relations).

What Melville accomplishes, then, is a preservation of reading, a deepening of the reader's (that is, his own, Ishmael's) relation with these texts. Ishmael, we recall, is a former schoolteacher; he makes indirect fun of himself by tweaking the lean-browed youth who "ships with the Phaedon instead of Bowditch in his head" (139; ch. 35). Knowing the text but not understanding it, he suffers awakenings both rude and slow as he moves ever more certainly toward insight. This deepening of reading is the pattern of Melville's own education, as nearly as can be established; and unfortunately it is just what American education on the whole, under the combined influence of Puritan schooling and the various classical revivals from Charles Eliot Norton to Mortimer Adler, has ignored: the negative dimension of Western literature, the way its most significant moments portray homecoming as not accomplished. But then classical education in America has scarcely had the relaxed position needed to reach for this depth; on the defensive in the face of a thorough-going utilitarianism, it has had to be compact and programmatic.

What *Moby-Dick* makes it possible to teach, therefore, is the need for the deepening of reading, for a life of encounters with great Western texts. Under Melville's guidance, this habitus reveals its importance for each person, not only for the professional scholars and other enfranchised sorts. The character of Ishmael the sailor undoes the disempowering American dichotomy of reader/doer. And as the notion of Western writing as monolithic authority comes undone, literature becomes an instrument for play, for banter, for refiguring. Rabelais, Burton, Browne and other writers of what Northrop Frye has designated the "anatomy" (*Anatomy* 313) and Mikhail Bakhtin the "Menippean" (87) emerge as tutelaries in this activity of reimagining oneself and one's cultural past and present.

But I suppose I need argue no longer to convince the teacher of this active intertextuality. The real problem remains of how to teach students, how to lead them into the habit of reading extensively, aggressively, and playfully in the texts of the past. Currently, reading seems to be a disappearing art: the economic pressures against a habit of reading have increased astronomically; the glamour of new technology has eclipsed its cultural image; and critics brandishing terms like "intertextuality" (although certainly there are worse ones) are making works less and less accessible even to competent readers.

Therefore it seems to me imperative that this MLA guide not be taken as a call to teach *Moby-Dick* as exemplifying critical principles. In graduate classes no doubt one ought to proceed to that level of inquiry, but undergraduates pose the problem of desire. In my experience there seem always to have been two classes of *Moby-Dick* readers among students: those who are disappointed-to-disgusted that it is not a straight adventure story and those (most often a smaller number) who revel in its play, its digressiveness and deferral. I have found that presenting a structure—while making it clear that the structure is not authoritative but heuristic—draws in many of the disaffected who have felt at sea, not realizing that they're experiencing what Melville intended (although, curiously, it never alleviates their distress to point out that they're experiencing it). The book of the white whale is the most notorious "loose baggy monster" in literature; to stake it out is perhaps to do it violence, but then, as Ishmael points out, by such violence are the lamps of the world lit—with whale oil.

The intertextuality of *Moby-Dick* plays out its chief drama: the fall of the West, which is "the end of the book and the beginning of writing" (or "writing/reading," to augment Derrida's phrase [3]); and this beginning leads to the second drama, the turning of Ishmael (largely through Queequeg, the "other" of Western civilization) into a text, a reader who is both writer and written on, a survivor of debacles and a storyteller in diasporic communities. And this drama takes me back to my first point, the transformative nature of Ishmael's experience.

I have found five stages in this process of turning or conversion in Ishmael, stages I designate as ironic (chs. 1–23), diagrammatic (chs. 24–48), Menippean (chs. 49–76), apocalyptic (chs. 77–105), and prophetic (ch. 106– epilogue) (see Cowan 77). Although I am quite attached to that diagram, taking the large view I concede that five may not be the final count on the structure of *Moby-Dick*. What determines my diagramming is finally what I stand by: that Ishmael is changed between the beginning and the end of his story; that he recognizes this transformation in retrospect, like Dante, while telling, not acting, his story; and that hence the varied rhetorical colorings of his language, the various tones of his voice, are crucial for the reader to distinguish, and all play a part in marking the dialectical movement of his inner voyage.

Ishmael's biting irony, his jocularity and frivolity, his high seriousness must first of all be felt and recognized by the student, by whatever means the teacher can muster. Beyond that experience of rhetorical power, however, it is important to see that these quickly shifting tones and moods— like the digressions and irrelevancies so often cursed by students—all lead somewhere and that one knows this primarily by the fundamental change in Ishmael. He is the dispossessed who is repossessed, the outcast who is gathered in, the accursed who is blessed—by nature, the divinity of the white whale, and the mourning and seeking human community of the *Rachel*.

Placing *Moby-Dick* in its historical setting for students must mean, then, not to overparticularize it in the whaling world of the 1840s but to lead them to see how it criticizes history itself. To read *Moby-Dick* successfully, for beginner or veteran, is to read critically. Melville's book is not merely a grand piece of work extolling the nobility of "Man" even in his delusion. It is a work of education, of scrutiny, of exclusion and selection; and its counsel can be felt even in a rudimentary reading. It is also, however, a work with the power to mold readers, and to become truly interested in it is to become a literary critic by brevet.

Toward *Moby-Dick*: A Freshman Honors Course*

Sanford E. Marovitz

One of the many qualities of *Moby-Dick* that make that novel so splendid and yet so difficult to teach to undergraduates is its intimidating comprehensiveness. An excellent approach I have found to accommodate that difficulty is to offer a wide-ranging course that uses Melville's magnum opus as a nucleus, the *principal* center of attention rather than the only one. I have employed this method successfully in what has become a favorite and rewarding experience teaching *Moby-Dick*, a two-semester (four credit hours each) freshman honors colloquium with fifteen students whose primary academic interests are in a variety of humanistic, scientific, and other professional areas of study. The Honors College at Kent State offers considerable flexibility to its instructors; consequently, I am free to teach the course in my own way and cover whatever material I think will be useful to students commencing their studies in higher education. In selecting *Moby-Dick* as the nucleus, I felt that anyone familiar with that novel and the multitude of sources from which Melville drew in writing it—directly and indirectly, consciously and unconsciously—would have acquired an excellent foundation for gaining more advanced knowledge and understanding in virtually any field of interest or endeavor. In this essay I wish in particular to address colleagues who enjoy similar flexibility in their own English programs and who may find a description of my aims and methods worth considering for those classes in which they have attempted to teach *Moby-Dick* and found themselves at times either swimming for their lives or else, like Pip, floating in the midst of "a heartless immensity" with their ringed horizons expanding around them miserably. Perhaps this description will illustrate at least one effective way to avoid such chartless voyaging in the future.

My course, Toward *Moby-Dick*, is essentially an introduction to humanistic literature in which Melville's novel is both a starting point and a goal. Most of the assignments are works with which Melville was familiar when composing it, as determined by internal and external evidence. We begin in the fall with Homer's *Odyssey*, read a few early Greek plays, several of the Platonic Dialogues (including the *Phaedo*), and relevant selections from the Bible. From there, temporal restrictions necessitate our making an enormous leap across the centuries to Dante's *Inferno*, Marlowe's *Dr. Faustus*, and an abridged edition of *Don Quixote*; I should like to add a selection from Rabelais next time I teach the course, but trying to decide what to

*I am indebted to Robert D. Bamberg, my colleague at Kent State, for reading an early draft of this essay and offering suggestions that led to its improvement.

eliminate in its favor leaves me feeling like Captain Delano with a knotful of loops and no ends to latch onto. The fall semester concludes with selected essays of Montaigne and two plays (regrettably there is time for only two) of Shakespeare—*Hamlet* and *King Lear*—both of which echo through *Moby-Dick* time and time again. We begin the spring term with major work of the seventeenth century, including most of *Paradise Lost* and a substantial selection from the writings of Sir Thomas Browne. I have assigned only *Gulliver's Travels* from the eighteenth century, though if time permitted, I should like to include portions of Boswell's *Life of Johnson*, which Melville purchased during his stay in London late in 1849 (and Ishmael does refer to it). From Coleridge I assign "The Rime of the Ancient Mariner" and a few chapters of the *Biographia*; from Carlyle, *Sartor Resartus*; and each student chooses a chapter from *On Heroes and Hero-Worship* to read and discuss in class. By this point we are just past mid-semester, and we shift to two major American writers—Emerson and Hawthorne—as our final preparation for cutting into *Moby-Dick*. The last three weeks of the semester are devoted entirely to that novel, and as relations between it and the past year's extensive reading become evident to the students, the effect on them of realizing how those correspondences have influenced the development of Ishmael's narrative becomes strikingly apparent. The class has reached a higher level of understanding.

At the beginning of the fall term I warn the students that it will be difficult to see the relations among all of the assigned works until they finally observe how Melville related them in *Moby-Dick*, and it is true that they occasionally become disturbed and disgruntled. But comments from the Honors College staff and several of the students testify to the overall success of the class; in fact, an advisor told me that students of past classes have requested that the course be continued on into the following year so that they might become still more comprehensive in their search for thematic and methodological influences and parallels. Clearly, they begin to see the pattern of associations and synergetic effects as soon as we come to *Moby-Dick* for a close reading.

Also at the beginning of the course, I ask the class to find time as soon as possible to read through the novel once quickly in order to see what it is like and what happens in the story. (Many of my students are vaguely familiar with the title and the roles of the major characters in the plot, perhaps from the film, but few have read *Moby-Dick* all the way through before entering college.) At that time I explain that we shall not discuss it until the last few weeks of the next semester—though I shall often allude to it where such references may be useful during the year, partly so that relevancies between it and the assignments will be made apparent and partly so that the students will retain it in the backs of their minds as the goal toward which they are gradually progressing. This method enables them to become at least somewhat familiar with the novel, familiar enough, that is, to recall it in relation to our daily discussions. When we finally come to it for analysis, the conjunction of so many theretofore obscure references into a meaningful pattern of recognizable allusions seems to generate astonishing intellectual excitement by opening up an entirely new mode of thought for most of the students; it is as if the muddied doors of perception were suddenly cleansed or, in Thoreau's words in the conclusion of *Walden*, as if those students had passed "an invisible boundary . . . and . . . will live with the license of a higher order of beings" (323–24). Of course, when this dynamic response occurs, the class is exciting for me, too; not only am I dealing at length and in depth with the one novel I most like to explore and teach, but I am also gratified over seeing how dramatically the students awaken to this sudden intellectual leap. It offers the kind of pedagogical experience and exhilaration that give most of us, on whatever level, our raison d'être, and it can never come too often.

In addition to writing three to five short papers each semester and a synoptic research paper at the end of the year (which also serves as a take-home final examination), each student is required to give one or two oral reports per semester on relevant topics chosen from lists I hand out early in the fall and spring. The lists comprise about two dozen subjects related directly or indirectly to the assigned reading material being discussed in class at the time; they generally pertain more to background information than to critical matters regarding the literature. But in compiling the lists I try always to ensure that they have some bearing on Melville's novel— though the relation may not be immediately discernible to the students. Nevertheless, because the choice of topics is wide and the students have a variety of academic and professional interests, they seldom have difficulty finding congenial subjects to investigate. With rare exceptions, they become more enthusiastic about their report topics as their probes into the material deepen, and by the time they present their observations and conclusions in class, they convey a sense of expertise.

What are the subjects on which I ask them to report? In the fall, I assign only one report, which deals generally with religion—Eastern and Western. A book that I require them to consult throughout the year—though we do not discuss it as an assigned text—is a volume of selections from major world scriptures; it serves as a starting point for the first report by providing students with enough browsing material to choose the area they wish to investigate in greater depth. (Both R. O. Ballou's *The Bible of the World* and Lewis Browne's *The World's Greatest Scriptures* are well suited to this purpose.) Students who wish to focus on a topic within the Judeo-Christian religions are expected to consult the King James Version of the Bible or some more recent translation as their primary source. Although one may complain that the major world religions and their scriptures, however divided among the class they may be, are far too vast individually and collectively to be encapsulated and discussed in fifteen brief oral reports, it will be well to remember two important things: first, most freshmen (and other undergraduates) have little or no knowledge of faiths and doctrines apart from the one in which they were reared (if any); and second, most crucial differences and similarities among the major religions are so pronounced that short, highlighted accounts of them are sufficient to help students make literary associations during the course generally and recognize relations between the sacred books and *Moby-Dick* in particular. If the knowledge they gain of individual religions and scriptures is regrettably superficial, the idea behind this method is to offer only a quick and, I believe, useful introduction, thereby opening new doors to further explorations and understanding, both in their own world and in the "wonder-world" of Melville's novel.

In the second semester I assign two oral reports rather than one. Again the topics suggested are large, but they are usually more precisely focused, and the first is clearly related to the historical background of early nineteenth-century America; consequently, the historical information the students present to one another through the reports will illuminate many aspects of *Moby-Dick* that would otherwise be left in the shadows. On the day of his or her report, the student distributes copies of the outline and a brief annotated bibliography of the principal sources used in gathering the information. Although I tell the class that they may select relevant topics other than those I have proposed for the first report of the term, nearly all choose their subjects from the list I hand out, which includes, for example, the higher biblical criticism in Germany, the great chain of being, American art and theater from 1825 to 1850, commercial whaling to 1850, the study of anatomy to 1850, the history of nautical cartography, gothic literature, and abolitionism in America.

Because the primary academic interests of the students in these colloquia are so diverse, I try to suggest topics that will help them relate their individual tastes and desires to the assigned readings and ultimately to Melville's novel. Of course, Ishmael himself makes this task relatively easy by introducing and associating an extraordinary range of materials in his narrative. The second oral reports are scheduled to begin as we move from British and European subject matter to American, and the topics have a direct bearing on the whale as a colossal "fluxional" symbol, as Emerson presents that term in "The Poet" and as Hawthorne illustrates it in his best fiction. I ask each student to choose an animal—natural, legendary, or mythic—and discuss it in relation to cultural history but with particular concern for its place in myth and legend. Thus a horse, for example, has a long history as a natural domesticated animal among many cultures, but there are also Pegasus, the

Trojan Horse, Rosinante, and the great "White Steed of the Prairies" to which Melville himself refers in *Moby-Dick* (165; ch. 42). The mermaid, Big-Foot, the Loch Ness monster, the serpent, the spider, the elephant, and so on are other creatures on which the students report (though leviathan is left for Ishmael alone), and the conjunction of all the mythic and legendary associations, especially with regard to actual animals, helps to give the class a sense of what the whale signifies in *Moby-Dick*. By understanding how we have traditionally humanized animals, the students are in a better position to see how effectively Melville has humanized his whale—and to realize why so many people who have been captivated by his novel have also become such impassioned members of the save-the-whales movement: the essence of Moby Dick lives and swims in them all.

Although occasionally during the year I assign short impromptu papers on pertinent issues of the times—racism, war, environmentalism, labor versus management, and others—at least one of the essays written outside of class each semester is based on an oral report for which the students have already done the preliminary research. In the first semester I ask them to relate the religion or scripture on which they have reported to one of the assigned authors or texts; this project enables them to anticipate the kind of literary relation they will be expected to make at the end of the year in reference to Melville's novel. In the second semester, I request that they convert their report on a legendary or mythic creature into a short research paper, thus preparing them for the final, more comprehensive project focusing on correspondences between *Moby-Dick* and the wealth of literature they have been studying throughout the year. If many of the ideas expressed in these final papers appear to be derivative, they are not always so, and they are nevertheless based on careful reading of all the primary work; moreover, such thoughtful investigation will often stimulate surprising insight in bright and diversified freshman students, even when they are dealing with profound and complex materials.

By the time the course has reached the point where daily reading assignments and class discussions on *Moby-Dick* begin, I have made numerous pointed references to the novel, and the students have already read it—albeit once and quickly—early in the first term. Therefore, I may reasonably assume that they are not moving into *Moby-Dick* "cold" and that although I may occasionally mention something unfamiliar to them (I consciously try to avoid such allusions), most of my questions and comments will touch on points, details, and correspondences to which they have already given some thought. They have had access to much of the extrinsic material pertaining to *Moby-Dick*, and realizing how Melville adapted, assimilated, and fused his sources in the novel through the "hell-fire" of his seething imagination is a great and sudden mind-opener for most of the class. The enthusiasm generated during the final three weeks when everything coalesces justifies the sporadic periods of frustration and sometimes despair that the students (and occasionally their teacher) have undergone while seeing each other three times a week for an entire year.

It is exactly because I place such faith in the success of those last weeks that I am so careful about assigning the novel day by day in consumable portions, even if it is necessary at times to bite into it sharkishly, chew rather quickly, and swallow chunks that are somewhat too large for thorough digestion. Apart from taking the novel chapter by chapter, giving it "much and earnest contemplation, and oft repeated ponderings, and especially by throwing open the little window towards the back of the entry" (20; ch. 3) for imaginative insight—all of which the students must learn to do on their own—there is no truly satisfactory way to cover *Moby-Dick* in segments. Like Ishmael, however, we attempt all things and achieve what we can. Because each instructor has his or her own points to emphasize in *Moby-Dick*, each will have to determine individually how much or how little to assign for the day, but one method that surely does *not* work well is dividing the novel into equal sections and assigning them on a strictly quantitative basis. Fortunately, *Moby-Dick* contains natural breaking points, cohesive and organic as it is; working according to them, the instructor can divide the book to accommodate almost any allotted number of class periods.

Before discussing the opening pages of the novel in detail, I take a little time to go over the plot and most obvious themes, emphasizing at first the story—the saga of a particular sea captain and his crew in desperate pursuit of a particular white whale. I like to point out that before and with—though certainly not above—everything else, Melville is a superb storyteller. Despite the excitement that the story generates, however, it is easy when dealing with *Moby-Dick* to disregard the action in favor of more esoteric fare once the first reading has been completed. One should not forget that in composing this novel Melville was still following up the great interest that had evolved in him at about the time he began drafting *Mardi* or shortly before—his desire to write a grand romance. And traditionally in a romance the story is the vehicle that carries everything else. To neglect it or pay it too little attention is as self-defeating as is attending to it exclusively, for in either case the wealth of cetological details and whaling lore that Ishmael provides, in attempting both to satisfy his own curiosity about the whale and to poeticize the whaling industry, will be left detached from the narrative framework. Consequently, all of that material will remain an unclassified "botch" (Hayford and Parker 558) of "constituents of a chaos" (117; ch. 32) instead of an oceanic harmony of parts contributing to the narrative as a whole. The very reality and solidity of those details constitute the basis of authenticity on which the romance is founded.

Also before addressing the opening day's assignment, I introduce the major figures briefly and generally but leave aside details of their thought, attitude, and behavior until the class reaches those points where Ishmael describes them. Ishmael as a character needs little more introduction than he gives himself in the first chapter, but as a narrator he requires some preliminary attention. I believe that it is wise to provide the students with enough information regarding the complex narrative point of view to help them recognize unexpected shifts and anomalies (e.g., Ishmael's knowing Ahab's most intimate thoughts and his occasional use of such dramaturgical methods as soliloquies, descriptions of scenes presented in the manner of stage settings, and dialogues with the speakers marked as on a script [chs. 37–40, 120–22]). Being prepared for such unexpected changes will enable the students to make better sense of them while reading; without this preparation relatively unsophisticated readers may be disturbed enough over the overt inconsistencies to succumb to bewilderment or frustration and simply disregard whatever is not immediately and superficially comprehensible.

In warning my students about the apparent changes in point of view, I also suggest that they try to notice the wide variety of styles Ishmael employs as he moves from chapter to chapter; from speaker to speaker; from the expository to the poetic; from the formal to the seaman's argot, the colloquial, the black vernacular (Fleece's sermon to the sharks), and pidgin English; from the wordplay of comedy and farce to the eloquent and highly charged expression of adventure and tragedy. By observing the variations in tone and diction while reading the novel instead of merely hearing about them afterward, the students may apprehend the microcosmic nature of *Moby-Dick* more effectually than they would through the outside aid of lectures or critical studies.

On commencing our close reading of the novel, I give disproportionate time to the preliminary pages ("Etymology" and "Extracts") and the first chapter, which together constitute my first day's assignment. I suggest that students go over those pages carefully—especially "Loomings," the opening chapter, because as Harrison Hayford has shown, it introduces many predominant themes and images that recur throughout the work, and one cannot devote too much attention to it. On the second day we take up nearly all of the semicomic, semimysterious narrative beginning (chapters 2–23). Here the relation between Ishmael and Queequeg is established and defined, the story moves forward, and the tone shifts from comic to ominous through such foreshadowings as the portentous Spouter-Inn painting (the description of which I discuss in detail in the light of Howard P. Vincent's remarks on it ["Ishmael"]), Father Mapple's sermon, and the appearance of Elijah. Also in this section, Ishmael anticipates the tragic grandeur of Ahab and his destiny. On the third day (chapters 24–42) Ishmael further aggrandizes his narrative with an epic aura. In addition to introducing Ahab, the crew, and the whale (folio to duodecimo), he illustrates (in "The Mast-Head") the wedding of meditation and water first mentioned in the opening chapter but juxtaposes it ominously with Ahab's monomania—his obsession for access to truth, vengeance, and victory over the evil that to him the white whale represents—all dramatically revealed in the two chapters following (ch. 36–37). "The Whiteness of the Whale" also warrants special attention for the manner in which it illustrates Melville's ambiguity, imagery, remarkable versatility with language, and assimilation of sources—the last of which is particulary noteworthy for this class. The fourth day's assignment is long and inclusive in comparison with most of the others, perhaps too long for us to do it justice, but it contains little that should cause the students great difficulty; in this segment I briefly highlight the main idea of several chapters ("The Chart," "The Mat-Maker," "The Hyena," "The Crotch," and "The Sphynx"), discuss the structural and thematic value of the gams, and show how Ishmael exposes human sharkishness (a topic so thoroughly and ably explored by Robert Zoellner). The fifth day (chs. 73–92) both allows us to consider further the philosophizing that Ishmael has begun in "The Sphynx" and more tightly conjoins whales to people, thus more subtly humanizing leviathan. The few chapters I assign for the sixth day (chs. 93–99) require considerable attention, and therefore I urge the students to reread them carefully before class. I believe that these chapters constitute the moral center of the novel, for they dramatize the crisis through which Ishmael must pass in order to stand apart from the rest of the crew (as he must because only through his solitary turning away from the Ahabian fire is his rescue as a lone orphan justifiable from a moral point of view). Ahab and the whale are seen in relation to each other in the next segment (chs. 100–10), which anticipates their mortal conflict on the third day of the chase; Ahab's monomania is further exposed as being at least in part sexually provoked, as is evident in the symbolic suggestiveness of emasculation in "Ahab's Leg" (ch. 106), and may thereby be related to both his fear of impotence with increasing age and his quest not only for ideality but for immortality as well. The oath and the storm in the eighth day's assignment (chs. 111–26) adumbrate through action and setting the coming climax, which is presented in the last day's reading through graphic description of awesome power. Ahab's quest has ended with his being bundled voicelessly into eternity, as a remark by Ishmael portends early in the novel (41; ch. 7). With Ahab's death many thematic conflicts have been left unresolved, and the lone Ishmael's rescue in the epilogue brings us back full circle to speculate on them and to summarize.

The last day allotted to discussion of *Moby-Dick* is usually the last day of the school year as well, apart from examination week, and I like to give the students that additional week's time to complete their final papers. To insist that the research papers be turned in on the final day of classes, before the students have had a chance to reconsider all their earlier course material in the light of their recent experience of poring over *Moby-Dick* section by section for the past three weeks—a culmination toward which everything for two semesters has been pointed—seems to me unfair to them and self-defeating for the instructor. Although I expect them to be well on their way with their papers even as they read through the novel, they surely need at least an additional several days to pull their thoughts and materials together into a clean, coherent, reflective, and readable paper.

One thing, however, that I do not ordinarily expect from these freshmen is extensive use of critical studies devoted specifically to *Moby-Dick*. I am far more interested in stimulating them to develop their own views on the basis of all that they have read during the year than I am in rereading the critics through their eyes. In class I deal holistically and organically not only with the novel itself but as much as possible with all of the reading that I have assigned; using this approach, I attempt to show how each of the classic literary works of nearly three millenia reflects as well as informs the writings that precede and follow it. When a student is interested in working on philosophical or other thematic relations between, say, the Bible or Plato or Shakespeare or Milton and *Moby-Dick*, then I suggest that he or she turn to the well-known studies of Nathalia Wright (*Melville's Use*) or Merton M. Sealts, Jr. (*Pursuing Melville*), or Charles Olson or Henry F. Pommer. But for the most part I believe that the excellent representative selection of critical pieces in the Norton edition of *Moby-Dick*, particularly when used in conjunction with the year's reading assignments, is fully adequate for my colloquium students. Good criticism is invaluable, of course, but only when used properly—that is, as agent, not principal—and few students at the outset of their collegiate studies have learned to employ it in this way. Therefore, in my colloquium I urge the students to permit the classics to shed light on each other, though I arrange the syllabus so that *Moby-Dick* receives beams at once from them all.

Although my experience using this format for a class has thus far been limited to the freshman level, I believe that the method is plastic enough to be adapted for equally valuable application in courses all the way up through the undergraduate and graduate years. Of course, the requirements would change according to the sophistication of the students, but the basic idea of employing knowledge about outside materials—that is, sources and influences—toward gaining a more profound understanding and appreciation of Melville's art in *Moby-Dick* is a viable one on any level of learning. It is comprehensive, synoptic, holistic; it plays on relations precisely as Melville did in nearly everything he wrote; and it requires reading the novel closely and carefully as well as associating external materials with it.

In any class that employs the format I have outlined in this essay, the instructor must be able to assume that the students are willing and able to go well beyond the usual expectations with respect to assignments. The reason should be obvious: a prodigious amount of comprehensive and yet careful reading is essential, and because the success of the class depends so heavily on the quality of the reports, the students are obligated to do a great deal of serious individual investigation, often in relatively or completely unfamiliar areas. But when one does have students who are truly prepared for a mind-stretching exercise of considerable duration, the rewards for them as well as for the instructor are immense. I know that from both testimony and experience. And I know, also, that by the time this essay appears in print I shall have started off another small group of freshman honors students on their magical, centripetal, three-thousand-year voyage toward *Moby-Dick*.

Teaching *Moby-Dick* to Non-English Majors

Steven Gould Axelrod

The Classroom Situation

I first read *Moby-Dick* in a large college English class designed for non–English majors. I remember being wrenched, drained, and shaken by the novel, as I was by no other work in the course. Eventually, I became an English major, read *Moby-Dick* again in graduate school, was moved again, and ultimately became a college professor, specializing in modern American poetry. I now find myself, from time to time, teaching exactly the kind of American literature course for nonmajors in which I first encountered Melville's great novel.

I do not remember much that my professor said about *Moby-Dick* twenty years ago. He was a kind and retiring man, somewhat apprehensive about the large crowds that this particular class drew—a sinless, open-faced Dimmesdale. I remember him hemming and hawing, mumbling something about the "two *Moby-Dick*s theory," and defending the cetology chapters on the grounds that such lore would have been lost had it not been preserved in literature. Such was the innocence of the 1960s. Literature could still be viewed as a means of preservation rather than an increasingly dispensable frill on a technological culture. Today one could plausibly argue that the cetology chapters may preserve the rest of the novel for biologists of the future. I do not recall that my professor said anything particularly distinguished about *Moby-Dick*, yet that first exposure had a tremendous impact on me, an impact that continues to affect my sense of the novel.

The present essay outlines some ideas about how a teacher can involve students in the novel and help them to understand and feel its particular power. But I think we should recognize that for many of our students we will be largely extraneous: the novel itself will do its work. All we need do is make sure that students read *Moby-Dick* with their pores open. In a sense, all the methods and procedures I propose aim for no more than that.

I focus my comments on teaching *Moby-Dick* to non–English majors, though my techniques can be selectively adapted for majors as well. Teaching literature to English majors is an easier task than teaching it to nonmajors. In every English class the majors take, they are exposed and reexposed to a paradigm for analytical reading. Whether that paradigm is traditional humanist, deconstructive, or something else does not much matter. The similarities that bind all current interpretive paradigms together are much stronger than the pale distinctions that divide them, even though it is always the distinctions that occupy us in our critical journals, professional meetings, and tenure disputes. When we teach *Moby-Dick*, or any literary work, we simply instruct our students to recall that basic paradigm (with whatever elaboration or emphasis happens to be our peculiar hallmark). In other words, English majors constitute, along with us, what Stanley Fish calls an "interpretive community," holding certain shared, continually reinforced assumptions about what a text is, how one derives meaning from it, and how one fits that meaning into larger contexts of signification.

The task for the teacher and students in the non-English-major class is more difficult. They must seek, somehow, to become an interpretive community in the space of ten or fifteen weeks. The teacher must do more than merely polish the borders of a cognitive structure already in place; he or she must help construct one from scratch. The actual interpretation of texts becomes less crucial than the interpretive modes that the class will learn. In other words, in the English class for nonmajors the act of interpreting *Moby-Dick* teaches not simply the novel but how to interpret as well—what categories to use and to what ends.

I don't believe that in such a class we should merely treat our students as imitation English majors or indeed seek to convert them into actual English majors (though that will in fact be the outcome for a small percentage of them, as it was in my own case). The general student's interest in literature differs significantly from that of the student planning to make a professional commitment to the field. If we truly think of literature as a broadly human rather than narrowly cultish activity, we must recognize that the former interest is just as legitimate and momentous as the latter. The kind of interpretive community we form in the class for nonmajors, therefore, will not be exactly the same as in the class for majors. Backgrounds and an awareness of current critical debate are less crucial to these students than are a sense of curiosity and an ability to achieve a degree of closure with a text. We should help them read with intellectual activity, emotional commitment, and a sense of independence, so that they do not feel they must rely on lecture notes to understand a novel or poem. We should ultimately train them not merely to "trust thyself," as Emerson has it, but to possess the skills and sense of purpose that justify such self-trust.

Moby-Dick is an ideal text to use with such goals in mind. It is one of the richest intellectual and emotional experiences available in American literature, and it dramatizes a quest for understanding and connection analogous to the one the students themselves undergo as they read the novel.

My Conception of the Novel

Before we move to some specific techniques I have used in teaching *Moby-Dick*, I would like to suggest my own conception of the novel, which underlies my pedagogical methods. I recognize, however, that my views are not universally shared. Those teachers who wish to teach a *Moby-Dick* that differs radically from my own may wish to revise my methods or to throw them out entirely and invent their own. In any case, the techniques I will outline are not fossilized truths but simply strategies that once worked for me.

With Richard Brodhead and others, I see *Moby-Dick* as a text that does not cohere, that does not make a monolithic proposition about reality— though it is much more than nothing. The book foregrounds certain questions and places them in selected contexts, even if it does not definitively answer them. It continually tests conceptions of reality and modes of representation, without ever fixing on any one of them. I use this view of the novel to encourage the openness that I think essential to the reading of all literature. *Moby-Dick* can itself be seen as a model of dynamic reading.

We can profitably relate *Moby-Dick* to other works of American fiction, especially to *The Scarlet Letter*. American fiction generally tends to subvert the expectations it elicits, tends to change its terms and contradict its own meanings. *Moby-Dick* subjects its plot, characters, themes, structure, and style to so many alterations and multiplications that it becomes exemplary. Instead of pretending to reproduce an origin, it reveals itself as a disjunctive collection of arbitrary signs; or, if we wish to move from Derrida to Bloom, it becomes "an image or lie of voice," an image of how an author and a system of literary signs struggle with each other (*Breaking* 4). Over the years, many valuable studies linking Melville and Hawthorne have appeared, ranging from Richard Chase's seminal account (*American Novel*) to recent works by Brodhead and John Irwin. Viola Sachs's more radical and problematical deconstruction also merits mention in this context, as does Edwin Eigner's thought-provoking analysis, which challenges some of Chase's premises but continues the tradition of connecting *Moby-Dick* to *The Scarlet Letter*.

It is equally helpful, however, to juxtapose Melville with Emerson. "I love all men who *dive*," Melville wrote to Evert Duyckinck, speaking of Emerson. And *Moby-Dick* shares this quality with Emerson's essays: the continual questing after knowledge. The novel exemplifies Emerson's ideal of "endless experiments" in its style, forms, and themes. Melville, like Emerson in "The American Scholar," supplies an image of "Man Thinking." Both writers are important because they exemplify the process of thinking rather than the achieved thought: "God keep me from ever completing anything. This whole book is but a draught—nay, but the draught of a draught" (128; ch. 32). For Emerson and Melville, once the thought was completed it became a prison, and the author had to begin once again the liberating process of thinking. Both writers came to share a sense that the imaginative search for truth was itself the ultimate human truth. Like Emerson in his later work, Melville's Ishmael finally learns to live with the lack of integrated vision, the gap between mind and thing.

Melville's Emersonian propensity to philosophize—to commence one speculation and, when that runs its course, to commence another—gives *Moby-Dick* great intellectual and emotional power, though it tends to diminish the usual strengths of the novel form: developed characterization and suspenseful plot. Characters make sense primarily as projections of other characters—Ahab and Queequeg as opposing sides of Ishmael, for example. Plot often gets swallowed up in philosophical speculation and cetology (which itself merges into philosophical speculation) and in interpolated tales that are themselves refractions of the same story and same philosophical issues. *Moby-Dick* uses its novelistic form to enclose a vast fantasia in which many genres and modes interweave in excited revery, undermining the claim of any one of them to represent reality completely by itself.

The ending is less an achieved vision than a momentary exhaustion of the urge to discover, though perhaps one can say that the movements from sea to land, solipsism to community, I-it to I-thou, and active adventure to the symbolic action of tale-telling (as indicated in ch. 54) all have some kind of privilege in that they do come at the conclusion of the narrative. The end is a resting place and a repression—a healthy one that restores not only the figure of Ishmael but the reader, after Ishmael's conflicts have been terribly exposed, recognized, and undergone.

Influenced by this view of the novel, I encourage my students to achieve intellectual process rather than sanctioned product. I seek to immerse them in an incredibly challenging and moving text. Their own experience should mimic the drama of *Moby-Dick* itself. Psychic anxiety, division, and obsession should eventually yield to mobility and freedom, to a sense that the brain has gone on a great journey and has proven itself capable of taking such a journey now and in the future.

Praxis

Out of a ten-week course in classic American literature, I usually allow a week and a half to two weeks for *Moby-Dick*. I find that many, probably most, of the students will have already read *The Scarlet Letter* or *Huckleberry Finn* at some point in their lives, but few will have previously read *Moby-Dick*, though some may have tried and failed. So we have two weeks or slightly less to introduce an immense—and immensely sophisticated—text to a hall filled with unpracticed and perhaps unwilling readers. One should not expect the world in such circumstances, but neither should one cynically or hopelessly expect nothing. I encourage students to read the whole book before the first class session but insist only on their having gotten through the first twenty-three chapters. Usually the first class session does not get past a general introduction and a close analysis of the initial pages. One has to enter the world of the novel a bit gingerly. I will generally ask the class how they are getting along with the reading and ask them about problems they are encountering. Often such questions lead to genuine discussion of issues in the text.

At the outset, students usually regard *Moby-Dick* as too heavy, slow, and dense. One class memorably hissed me when I announced on the first day that they would have to read the whole book. I mitigate this problem by permitting them to skim through the cetology chapters, which I list for them. I want to prevent the novice readers from getting bogged down in the middle third of the novel, and, furthermore, I find that it helps them to have the essaylike chapters explicitly distinguished from the more traditionally fictional ones. But more important, I allow the students to express their legitimate reluctance to read such a difficult and intimidating book. When I keep the lines of communication open between the class members and me, their attitudes usually undergo a transformation. Almost all of them, of whatever level of accomplishment, end up respecting the book; and many end up loving it. For such students, *Moby-Dick* is dreadful in prospect but pleasurable in retrospect. If you just get a student into the book, relatively free of guilt and anger, Melville will take over and accomplish his magic.

No matter how large the class, I encourage discussion of the book, focusing on both individual passages and larger issues. I make sure that we analyze chapters I consider crucial (e.g., 1–13, 23, 36–38, 40–42, 93, 99, 133–35), but I let student interest dictate our focus a minority of the time. I use such devices as choosing four or five students to come up to the blackboard— usually slightly against their will—and asking them several critical or affective questions that they can answer briefly: Who is the hero of the book? What are two or three important images in the book? Why does Starbuck fail to rebel? Is the novel antiwhale? What is the point of the Radney-Steelkilt story? What is the central theme of the book? What single word best sums up the book (or a specific chapter or character)? and, simply, Do you like the book? Students at their desks are encouraged to write their own answers to the questions, and then a general discussion ensues on the basis of answers written on the board and at students' desks. I try to keep the class ambience supportive and good-humored, as well as intellectually serious.

The likelihood of a vast dissimilarity among answers and of naive and even "wrong" answers is not a problem but an advantage. The process forces cards that are usually hidden onto the table for discussion. To the question about the book's hero, I have usually received a variety of responses: Ahab, Ishmael, Queequeg, Moby Dick, sometimes even Starbuck or a wild card like Pip or Stubb. (I have yet to receive a suggestion that the text itself is its own hero.) Sometimes an obvious choice is omitted—recently, this has happened with Ahab—and that omission becomes a useful discussion starter. At other times, there will be a vigorous dispute among partisans of different figures. In the debate, students develop more sophisticated opinions, abandon indefensible positions, sharpen their ability to form persuasive critical arguments, gain confidence in their ability to understand a difficult text on their own without their teacher telling them what to think, and strengthen their sense of themselves as a lively and cohesive intellectual community.

Of course, the teacher must decide whether to intervene in the discussion and to what degree. My basic premise is that if useful things are being said, if the conversation is getting somewhere, I should stay out of it as much as possible. It is more valuable for the students to arrive at an idea themselves than for the teacher to give it to them. At other times, however, when the discussion gets seriously off track or becomes redundant, I step in with a question or a summary of what's been said, in order to get things moving again. I am apt to point out larger implications of the discussion at hand— how, for example, one's identification of the hero relates to one's sense of the novel's theme, structure, and purpose. Sometimes class discussions end in a consensus, with the better ideas having driven out the worse. More often, the class will remain divided. While I allow a consensus to develop if one seems to be looming, I am not afraid to conclude a discussion without one. Although too many loose ends may lead to a demoralizing sense of futility, too few imply a packaging of responses, a false unanimity, a flight from the multiplicity of reality. Besides, it often takes time for better opinions to drive out the worse, for light to dawn. Students will continue to think about the issues raised long after the discussion is concluded; they may raise the issues anew at the next session.

Another method I use is to pose a question to the class and write students' responses briefly on the board, being careful to inject no words of my own. I then ask the class as a whole to discuss the responses, perhaps to refine them, change them, expand them, or simply affirm them. The board gets covered with terms and phrases, many of which get crossed out and revised or just crossed out. In the process, a student who made an initial response may well volunteer his or her own substitution or refinement. In this way, I encourage the class as a whole to think.

At some point toward the end of the novel, I ask students to write briefly what they like best and dislike most about *Moby-Dick* and then ditto up the responses for general distribution. This procedure helps validate the ideas and feelings of novice readers. Although I reproduce the comments in random order, I make some attempt to group the responses in class discussion, to show that the class seems to share some common lines of thought. For example, many comments about the "best" aspect of the book revolve around the characters:

Melville's Ishmael carries me along with him in philosophy and experience. I "feel" the voyage.

Queequeg. Relationship with narrator. Ideas he helps convey about accepting others who are different.

The relationship between Ishmael and Queequeg—the love and "fellowship" that they shared.

Ahab's obsession.

The characters and the witty way they are portrayed.

Others point to themes:

Brotherhood.

The point he makes that cultures may be different but not superior or inferior.

The best thing about *Moby-Dick* is that there are a lot of interesting things about whaling.

The idea that a person has to find the meaning of his life, what is it all for?

I think one of the most important points of *Moby-Dick* is that Melville questions death.

Still others point to aspects of style and form:

The author's use of symbolism in using various whaling tales, descriptions of whaling and Moby Dick specifically to show Ahab's struggles against his inner being.

The symbolism and themes are very well thought out and planned.

Endless symbolic possibilities.

The best thing is the book's humor. It sheds a brilliant quality on the book.

The best thing is the little jokes everywhere (some are really funny), and the way he plays with the reader's mind—never answering questions, and at times, contradicting himself.

The best thing about *Moby-Dick* is Melville's writing style—the way he uses language to express feelings.

The descriptions, the action, and story line.

And finally, there are the inevitable naysayers:

The book supported him long enough to write "Bartleby" and "Billy Budd."

No opinion.

The list of the book's worst features is also valuable. The large majority complains about its length and about the "time and concentration" it requires. Several complain about what they take to be its endorsement of whale killing. This objection provides an opportunity to examine the novel's rhetoric concerning whales: the movement from an Ahab-like assertion of their malevolence and otherness to a more accurate sense of their enigmatic yet not unkind behavior, the movement from hatred to respect and even love (see Zoellner).

Most often I will begin a class session with lecture material, which I intend as a model for thinking about a text. This part lasts perhaps twenty minutes. I might speak about the relation of the novel to other works we have read in the course—*The Scarlet Letter* or Emerson's essays, for example. I might try to place *Moby-Dick* more generally in American literary tradition or in the context of its times, its composition history, or Melville's life and canon. I might mention some of the novel's central concerns: the enigma of reality; the limitations of the symbolizing process; the search for metaphysical truth apart from mediating conventions and institutions; the quest for love and human connection; the relation of culture to nature (exemplified in the changing depictions of whales); the dialectic of solipsism and community; the child's search for its father, the related theme of exile, and the countertheme of demonic defiance; the absurd, the grotesque, and existential nausea; the critique of hierarchy and totalitarian power; original sin, human depravity, and radical evil; the limits of reason; fate versus free will, and so on.

In the later stages of the class session, I withdraw more into the background, functioning as a facilitator, and let the class lecture to me or to itself. Instead of divorcing myself emotionally from the students, however, I try to remain an engaged presence—especially when they solicit information or opinion from me—and a good listener. But as the hour proceeds I volunteer less and only as the occasion arises, rather than in the coherent, prepared format of my initial lecture. I attempt to be humorous, intellectually intense, and flexible. On some occasions, for variety's sake, I may proceed differently: I may begin the class hour with a question, or with students at the blackboard, or by simply reading the novel aloud.

The next time I teach *Moby-Dick* I will undoubtedly try some new ideas. Perhaps I will ask students to keep a journal (leaving them free to write whatever they wish: a running commentary, an analysis or evaluation, a parody, a meditation) or to copy out favorite sentences from the novel. I may, as I have in the past, ask them to write a short paper analyzing the artistry of a paragraph of their choice or comparing the paragraph to one in, say, *Walden* or *The Scarlet Letter*. The object is to keep the menu reasonably fresh, to remain committed to the class, and to encourage the students to strengthen their connection to Melville's novel. I regard the final exam not merely as an occasion for separating those who write proficiently about the text from those who write less proficiently but also as an opportunity for students to sum up their ideas about the book; it can provide the satisfaction of momentary closure.

My teaching is partly intuitive, partly modeled on my own best teachers, and partly learned in the abstract. (Barrett Mandel's essay on teaching literature comes to mind here as being influential.) Over the years I have found that some students prefer the passive role of transcribing lecture material without having to respond or initiate. So I make it a point at the outset of the course to describe my modus operandi and invite those who would prefer another to seek out an alternative class. Although few students leave as a result, such a declaration seems to make class members feel that they have made a conscious choice to undergo the experience and hence are responsible for what ensues. I want students to know that they have power over the class, as they have over texts—and that my power is ultimately designed to increase their own.

As teachers we need to be pragmatic, using whatever seems to work and not getting in the way of the book and the students. Whatever our methods, our goal must always be to encourage stronger reading. The most important thing I can do in teaching *Moby-Dick* is to open students up to the intellectual life as I understand it, to what Harold Bloom calls "love for a text" (*Agon* 329), and to one of the most inventive and powerful texts there is.

Teaching *Moby-Dick* in a Calvinist Setting

Kathleen Verduin

I first read *Moby-Dick* at sixteen, in the old Random House edition with the beautiful austere engravings by Rockwell Kent. Though it is easy to distort these experiences in retrospect, I think I felt what Melville might have understood as a shock of recognition: the book seemed to belong to me in some mysterious and private way. It was partly the solemnity of the actual volume, the covers black as the Bible, the equally biblical starkness of the illustrations; but the text also absorbed me, to a degree that I found a little scary. My father told me at the time that he had read *Moby-Dick* as a boy—and liked it; that too was memorable, since I never knew him to read novels and in those days he rarely spoke of his inner life.

It seems to me now that my reaction to *Moby-Dick* was almost inevitable and that I unconsciously recognized in it the Calvinist aura of my youth. Growing up on the outskirts of a Dutch Reformed enclave south of Chicago, I had undergone my elementary education at an institution named for John Calvin; I suffered my first crisis of faith in the third grade, when my class was formally introduced to the doctrine of Predestination; I had no little experience with men and women firmly convinced of their Election. But I also sensed, just as clearly, an intensity of purpose and a mood of cosmic drama, and I loved the continual exposure to the Bible, especially the Old Testament with its stories of love and death and vast spaces. All these memories were strangely present to me in *Moby-Dick*. As an undergraduate at Hope College in Holland, Michigan, an institution founded by Dutch Calvinists in the nineteenth century, I later studied Melville under James Prins—a gaunt, impassioned teacher who, to compound matters, reminded me on certain rainy days of Rockwell Kent's Ahab. Prins made Ahab live, perhaps because he too was a man in an eternal attitude of protest—against injustice, against the inauthentic, and more often than not against the Dutch Calvinism that had shaped and, clearly, scarred him.

My present position as an instructor at my alma mater has forced me to relive much of my own past, particularly with regard to Calvinism and to those friends and teachers who helped me explore and come to terms with it. Hope College is by no stretch of the imagination a militantly Calvinist institution: most of my students hold religious ideas that are vague, sanguine, and comfortable, and more than a few of them may think Calvin is a character in, say, the Book of Acts. For others, however, Calvinism is still a potent force, even—as perhaps for Melville—an adversary. Among the responses I elicited from students, several were classic: "Just the word 'Calvinism' makes me angry," confessed one young woman. "The idea of predestination or the belief that some are chosen (for salvation) and some are not is portrayed as: *We* (the Dutch Reformed Church) are chosen; *you* are not. Whatever

John Calvin may have meant by those and other doctrines, the church I was raised in used them as excuses for cruelty and exclusivity." Another wrote, "Maybe I don't understand the theological implications of Calvinism to the ultimate degree, but to me Calvinism is not simply the dos and don'ts but the attitude of total depravity—the continuous fear of God and insecurity in oneself." Still another, whose childhood included Wednesday night catechism but no Sunday television, agreed that Calvinism was "a foundation for prejudice" and added darkly, "I believe it could be a dangerous weapon in the wrong hands."

To the outsider, these statements must sound like something right out of the nineteenth century. But they express the tensions with which many of my students continue to struggle, in patterns laid down for them by generations of ancestors. The Dutch-American film director Paul Schrader has displayed a similar anachronistic resentment in *Hard Core*, where (no doubt for the first time on the screen) the Five Points of Calvinism are recalled, recited, and subjected to the indignity of the adolescent prostitute's incredulous response, "And I thought *I* was fucked up!" The religious climate at Hope and the frequently obsessive guilt of some students (often expressed in nervous jokes about guilt, depravity, and Original Sin) thus provide a context particularly suitable for a discussion of *Moby-Dick* and its relation to Calvinism. Though the six sessions spent on it in my course in the American novel necessarily cover many aspects of the book—its characters, its allegorical method, its place in the romantic tradition, it significance for the genre—I do try to devote at least one or two sessions to an investigation of Melville's supposed Calvinism, and I include the subject among the essay topics I distribute later.

Melville's religious views have of course been discussed since the early years of the Melville revival, especially by Henry A. Murray ("In nomine diaboli"), Lawrance Thompson, and William Braswell. In the last decade or so, perhaps reflecting the rise of scholarship on Puritanism, several significant studies have appeared. A perceptive and stately essay by Thomas Werge, "*Moby-Dick* and the Calvinist Tradition," places Melville's work in the context of passages from Calvin and several seventeenth-century Puritan divines, concentrating on what Werge terms the epistemological problem of the novel. T. Walter Herbert, Jr., in Moby-Dick *and Calvinism: A World Dismantled*, explores in detail the Dutch Reformed Church of Melville's childhood, especially as it was embattled against religious liberalism, and interprets Melville's reaction to his father's mental collapse and death. Herbert also discusses the Calvinist implications of Father Mapple's sermon and Ahab's revolt, and he liberally documents his study with quotations from Calvin and nineteenth-century Calvinist theological works. Extremely provocative is the all-too-short section (289–326) on *Moby-Dick* in Ann Douglas,

The Feminization of American Culture; equally stimulating is William H. Shurr, *Rappaccini's Children: American Writers in a Calvinistic World.* Shurr argues that Calvinism—or what American writers have, in the words of Twain, "taken to be calvinism" (12)—is indeed the American national religion; his discussion of *Moby-Dick,* "a compendium of what our native calvinism can be" (142), is the climax of his study. As with all the sources I will quote in this essay, I find passages from these critics useful for distribution; coming not directly from me but from published sources, these materials help focus the ideas I want to present, making them, I suppose, more authoritative and less contingent (see also Wright, *Melville's Use,* and Pommer).

In my lecture, then, after inviting preliminary responses on the subject of Calvinism, I present as concisely as I can the Five Points of Calvinism outlined by the Synod of Dordt in 1618–19: Total Depravity, Unconditional Election, Limited Atonement, Irresistible Grace, Perseverance of Saints (the "tulip" acronym can be savored in a Dutch community). Certain passages bear quotation in full, especially those regarding the doctrine of Predestination:

> That some receive the gift of faith from God, and others do not receive it, proceeds from God's eternal decree. . . . According to which decree He graciously softens the hearts of the elect, however obstinate, and inclines them to believe; while He leaves the non-elect in His just judgment to their own wickedness and obduracy. And herein is especially displayed the profound, the merciful, and at the same time the righteous discrimination between men equally involved in ruin; or that decree of election and reprobation, revealed in the Word of God, which, though men of perverse, impure, and unstable minds wrest it to their own destruction, yet to holy and pious souls affords unspeakable consolation.   (*Canons of Dordt* 98; ch. 1, art. 6)

For some students, this perspective is entirely new and strange; others, though, were weaned on it, and they are generally eager to express themselves at this point. We discuss the doctrine's paradoxical nature and the cosmic questions it provokes; then, for Calvin's own reaction to such questions, we look at the following passage from the *Institutes* (drawn to my attention by Werge's study):

> Of the immensity of God's judgments you have the clearest evidences. You know that they are called "a great deep." Now, examine your contracted intellects, whether they can comprehend God's secret decrees. What advantage or satisfaction do you gain by plunging your-

selves, by your mad researches, into an abyss that reason itself pro-
nounces will be fatal to you? Why are you not at least restrained by
some fear of what is contained in the history of Job and the books of
the prophets, concerning the inconceivable wisdom and terrible power
of God? . . . Do you seek reason? I will tremble at the depth. Do you
reason? I will wonder. Do you dispute? I will believe. I see the depth,
I reach not the bottom.   (414; bk. 3, ch. 23, sec. 5)

These passages help establish the doctrinal background and the mood of
Calvinism, and once I have pointed out Melville's own connection with the
Dutch Reformed Church, his interest in theology, and the references to
Calvin and Calvinist doctrines in *Pierre, Clarel,* and *Billy Budd,* we are
ready to look at the novel itself. The Calvinism of *Moby-Dick* is first evident,
I point out, in the biblical allusions, especially the personal names—Elijah,
Ishmael, Ahab, Rachel—more frequently chosen from the Old Testament
than from the New. We turn then to chapter 9, the famous sermon of Father
Mapple. I find that many students are surprised to encounter a sermon in
a novel; in their minds, the two forms have about as little to do with each
other as Athens with Jerusalem, and it was not too long ago that I myself
was warned by a well-meaning minister not to read *Tess of the d'Urbervilles.*
Yet sermons are often the only form of rhetoric that some students have
experienced outside the classroom; fairly regularly their own papers slip into
sermonal patterns, adopting admonitory tones and moralistic conclusions.
Mapple's sermon thus engages their attention: it reminds a few of the film
version, which featured Orson Welles in the role, but for others it is un-
comfortably familiar, the kind of thing they've heard all their lives. We
consider Mapple's belief that "If we obey God, we must disobey ourselves"
(45). This tenet can stir some interesting discussion between Calvinist students and others who find Mapple's statement shocking. "Is this supposed
to be funny?" asked one lapsed Unitarian. Another found a disturbing parallel
between Mapple's self-suppression and breaking a horse.

I try to place the sermon in a larger, historical context: Mapple's words,
as veterans of my American literature survey recognize, reverberate with
Puritanism, and a comparison between his sermon and one preached by
Samuel Danforth (1626–74) at the grave of his own children proves how
deftly Melville has caught the Calvinist tone: "It is the pleasure of God, that
(besides all that may be gain'd by reading, and studying, and preaching)
I should learn and teach obedience by the things that I suffer. The holy
fire is not to be fetcht for you, out of such a flint, as I am, without smit-
ing . . . " (qtd. in Mather 2: 53). I show that Mapple's metaphors of father-
hood and sonship resemble those repeatedly employed by Joseph Bellamy
(1719–90), the New England theologian most useful for evoking the distor-

tions and rigidity characteristic of Calvinism in Melville's time:

> It is an honor that belongs to God, to govern the world which he has made; to govern his world; to lay out and order the affairs of his own family. We think we have a right to lay out schemes for our own families, and should take it ill if our children or servants should dispute our right. . . . Much more has God a right to lay out an universal plan, for the conduct of all things, in a world to which he has an original, underived, absolute right; nor can he look upon the worm that dares dispute his right, but with infinite contempt and detestation.   (Bellamy 2: 94)

But it is obviously more important to explore the psychological implications of Mapple's worldview, which culminates not in resignation but in transfiguration:

> And eternal delight and deliciousness will be his, who coming to lay him down, can say with his final breath—O Father!—chiefly known to me by Thy rod—mortal or immortal, here I die. I have striven to be Thine, more than to be this world's, or mine own. Yet this is nothing; I leave eternity to Thee; for what is man that he should live out the lifetime of his God?   (51; ch. 9)

"What's in it for them?" asked a perplexed student whose Spanish surname marked her as rather far beyond the pale of Dutch Calvinism. "All this reminds me of the tenets of the Party in *1984*, things like 'Freedom is Slavery.' . . . It's like saying 'Suffering is Happiness.' If God is like this, why do you need a devil?" However spontaneous, her question was particularly appropriate to the religious traditions at least dimly familiar to many of my students. In *The Blood of the Lamb*, describing the Chicago Dutch of his childhood, novelist Peter DeVries notes ironically,

> These displaced Dutch fisherfolk, these farmers peddling coal and ice in a strange land, must have had their reasons for worshipping a god scarcely distinguishable from the devil they feared. . . . All the theologies inherent in the minister's winding drone came down to this: Believe in God and don't put anything past him.   (25)

My student's question was the kind of authentic response every teacher wants. But such questions always jar me a little and make me once again aware how hard it is to teach a work with personal significance. I hear myself saying something about the drama of it all, the excitement of being caught up in a cosmic wrestling match with the Almighty. I remember Ann Douglas's remark about Bellamy's conception of God: though in many ways horrifying, she acknowledges,

> it clearly once possessed immense imaginative and intellectual appeal. Unfair as it undoubtedly is, it operated as a model of majesty; crushing, humiliating as it may appear and often was, it could be a source, almost uniquely so among Western religions, of energy. It provided its adherent, no matter how it belittled him, with a supreme and commanding object of worship. (123)

But insightful as such a passage is, it inevitably falls short of capturing the reality it seeks to define. What does this have to do with my mother's sudden death, when my father, with no self-consciousness at all, spoke sincerely of the comfort he drew from the Calvinist doctrine of the Sovereignty of God? As an academic and a student of Puritanism, I make a quick connection with the *Personal Narrative* of Jonathan Edwards: "The doctrine of God's sovereignty has very often appeared an exceeding pleasant, bright and sweet doctrine to me: and absolute sovereignty is what I love to ascribe to God" (Levin and Gross 324). But I feel a guilty sense that I am betraying people I love. Like many of them, Father Mapple cannot lightly be dismissed as a hypocrite; like theirs, his convictions are not easily viewed as rationalizations. On the contrary, his sense of personal fulfillment is obvious and radiant.

"Is there—paradoxically—well, something *beautiful* about this doctrine?" I venture tentatively. These are dangerous waters: constrained by filial piety, I also run the risk of capitulating to the enemy, of siding with others against my students (my air of complicity with whom has been cited as one of my pedagogical strengths). But they seem to understand. We talk of Moby Dick as a possible incarnation of a Calvinist God. Primordial, powerful, and entirely self-sufficient, the white whale is a perfect example of Sovereignty; he has, moreover, a "predestinating head" (468; ch. 135) and is, like Jehovah, unknowable. "Dissect him how I may," confesses Ishmael, "I go but skin deep; I know him not, and never shall" (318; ch. 86). Cetology, whose importance for the novel has been firmly established, thus resembles the meticulous anatomizings of theological treatises, dogged but myopic attempts to apprehend inaccessible deity (see Ward and Greenberg). And like the Calvinist God, Moby Dick seems by turns benign and malevolent, sublimely transcending moral imperatives.

Yet the whale also invokes a universal and primitive pattern, nature as a medium for the numinous and divine. We spend some time on chapter 42, Melville's great meditation "The Whiteness of the Whale." Having found unexpected parallels to Melville's central symbol in a modern novel, I pass around one or two quotations from Dirck VanSickle's *Montana Gothic*, where the injured eagle, in its majestic indifference, resembles Moby Dick and comes as close as anything I know to what Calvinists may mean by the Sovereignty of God:

> The bird was manifestly a creature of power, but the power was amoral—unlike Deke's, whose life had been weighed on the balance taught him in childhood, all his acts and even thoughts judged for signs of good and bad. . . . the bird just lay on its back, watching as if calmly mocking the man's puny efforts to assault its citadel, as Deke thought of the eagle: an alien fortress of concentrated being.   (60, 62)

I ask that my students enlarge their ideas of religion to see that it comprehends the awesome as well as the consoling and accommodates profoundly ambivalent emotions. I distribute excerpts from Rudolf Otto's classic study of the psychology of religion, *The Idea of the Holy*, passages where Otto describes the concept *mysterium tremendum et fascinans* (12–13). It is this otherness, this ambiguity, this unknowability, this melding of horror and glory, I contend, that so fixes and fascinates the reader who contemplates the whale—and that held and continues to hold so many reluctant Calvinists.

Father Mapple, observed one student, is the kind of man Ahab could have been "if he could just have let go of all that anger." "I thought of the isolation of both of them," said another, "the way Mapple pulls his ladder up after him." Both figures are intense, heroic, and absorbed in one idea, and they are clearly juxtaposed. If *Moby-Dick* is at least on one level a novel rising from Calvinism, if the white whale may be seen as a fitting incarnation of the Calvinist God, then Mapple and Ahab present two opposing reactions. Calvin's "Do you reason? I will wonder" prefigures Mapple's submission, the submission from which he nevertheless derives his force. William Scheick's excellent introduction to *The Life and Death of That Reverend Man of God, Mr. Richard Mather* might be a commentary on Mapple; Scheick notes the "collective voice" of successive generations of Puritan fathers, the power engendered by suppression of individual identity and absorption into the archetype (7–21). To speak with the voice of the fathers, as Mapple does, is to speak with authority; to superimpose one's will on the will of God is to unite with the inexorability of the greater being. Hence, I think, Mapple's peculiar impressiveness, his patriarchal stature. Ahab is the obverse of Mapple: where Mapple submits to the rod, Ahab hurls himself against it and embodies the "mad researches" against which Calvin warned. The captain's struggles against the doctrine of Predestination are well known: "Is Ahab, Ahab? Is it I, God, or who, that lifts this arm? . . . By heaven, man, we are turned round and round in this world, like yonder windlass, and Fate is the handspike. . . . Who's to doom, when the judge himself is dragged to the bar?" (445; ch. 132). Yet he is also a believer, insisting, "This whole act's immutably decreed" (459; ch. 134). If Ahab is in revolt against Calvinist orthodoxy, he is also unable to define himself except in relation to it. Ann Douglas is right, I think, in saying that Ahab "cannot be understood without some knowledge of Calvinism" (305), and Herbert's comments on Ahab and predestination ring true: "If a man's eternal destiny and his everyday actions are determined by decrees set forth before the world was created, then human life becomes a 'mere mechanical' working out of what has already been decided . . . what is dramatized is Ahab's struggle to lay claim to his own life" (142).

Now and then a student has the acuity to wonder whether Ahab really loves Moby Dick. Said one, "He'd almost choose the whale over life without the whale." We discuss chapter 132, "The Symphony," and appreciate its beauty. "But I think if Ahab went back to his wife and child he'd just vegetate," confessed one student (herself a young wife; did it cost her something to say this?). "I didn't even like reading about it. It wasn't consuming, it wasn't love. . . ." The whale has given Ahab's life meaning, and in a sense he dies at last united with it, in a parody of embrace. And though ultimately self-destructive, his revolt invests him with a stature made heroic by the dimensions of his adversary. Like DeVries, whose novels endlessly explore the same pattern, the same confrontation between religion and irreligion, like Schrader, whose films so often seem a self-conscious indulgence in forbidden games (perhaps matched by a former teacher's dismissal of Schrader as "naughty"), Ahab simply can't let it alone. I think of my student whose parents (like mine) forbade Sunday television in a futile attempt to keep the world at bay. He never turned in a paper; he rarely deigned to attend class. When he was present, he tended to draw the discussion to such reprobates as Nietzsche. If in a lower key than Ahab's, his revolt was equally absorbing and equally destructive, yet somehow a course he had to follow: perhaps his own struggle to lay claim to his own life. That he was willing to offer a comment on Calvinism I take as significant.

"I get to wondering how much the whale was just an excuse," said one student; "did Ahab always feel this kind of anger and just find something to place it on?" The question suggests another: Was Melville's own engagement with Calvinism "just an excuse," a convenient target for rage more psychological than religious in origin? Ultimately, is it fair to define Melville in sectarian terms? Herbert argues that in *Moby-Dick* Melville "dismantles" a theocentric system and is then "left with the fear that no way of ordering consciousness remained" (175). Shurr finds Ishmael "the first of us to liberate himself from the national religion" (140). As another critic counters, however,

Melville did not leave these ideas behind in *Moby-Dick*; indeed, he immersed himself in them in his next novel, *Pierre* (1852) (see Milder, "'Knowing,'" esp. 98–101). Clearly Melville was not an orthodox Calvinist, as he was not an orthodox Christian; even the Calvinist influences he encountered in youth were already residual fragments, counteracted by other systems of thought. Yet Calvinism provided him with a set of doctrines and perhaps an emotional climate that organized his experience and answered the needs of his imagination. It was a ready image, still sufficiently pervasive in his culture—as with a slightly different face it is for me and my students—for its *disjecta membra* to reassemble like dry bones in life's more sober moments. One thinks of Chillingworth's words in *The Scarlet Letter*: "My old faith, long forgotten, comes back to me, and explains all we do, and all we suffer" (174; ch. 14).

Obviously, I feel justified in presenting *Moby-Dick* not only as a great work of American literature but as a model in which my still-Calvinist students may confront their own religious struggles at an artistic distance and as a means for others in the course to understand an unfamiliar tradition. A sensitive student new to Holland was inspired to do further research on Melville as a way of gaining insight into the community in which she found herself, and I find her impressions eloquent and gratifying:

> What is so sad is that while such a man as Herman Melville had the wherewithal to deal with the dilemmas of such a repressive religion, many members of this community barely grasp the implications and conflicts such concepts as total depravity of man, election of an elite to eternal salvation, predestination, and so forth, pose to men who believe in them. . . . Studying *Moby-Dick* or any literature in which men challenge religion's or society's definitions of Truth may be the only therapy, the only door men have to their own minds, particularly in communities such as this one. As painful as it is to follow Melville through a novel such as *Moby-Dick*, it is also emancipation for those who have no other outlet to recognize how elusive the Truth can be.

What I hope for my own students is that they will leave *Moby-Dick* knowing something about their religious heritage and perhaps about themselves and that they will find in Melville a brother. If the novel's significance were confined to colleges like Hope and communities like Holland, this essay would hardly deserve a place here, but to understand *Moby-Dick* in the light of Calvinism is also to be in touch with a spirit that has pervaded American literature since the seventeenth century. As Shurr has pointed out, "Calvinism has provided a highly charged myth of the culture: its multifaceted imperatives and taboos have produced the sharp edges that distinguish American authors and their works from those of any other culture" (144). Melville, indeed, understood Calvinism as a form of humanity's archetypal apprehension of good and evil, one "from whose visitations, in some shape or other, no deeply thinking mind is always and wholly free" (Hayford and Parker 540).[1]

NOTE

[1]Several students were helpful to me in the preparation of this essay, but I am especially grateful to Jacqueline Bartley, Eric Brummel, Mark and Lisa Lankton-Lenzo, Christine Pickering, Elizabeth Schilling, and Deborah Torres.

Class Conflicts in Teaching *Moby-Dick*

David Leverenz

Like any state university, Rutgers draws most of its students from middle- and working-class backgrounds. For many of them, *Moby-Dick* looms as the great unreadable American novel. They're likely to have had little experience with the mind play that Ishmael dotes on and only a vague exposure to cultural traditions that Melville takes for granted: Shakespeare, the Bible, public oratory, philosophy, mythology. I used to think that their resistance simply reflected a limited access to elite styles of learning. I assumed that a major part of the teacher's role should be to fill in some of the gaps. Recently, however, I've come to think that student difficulties with Melville's text imply more basic conflicts in values.

Some students, perhaps the majority, like the narrative's more practical and social aspects: the adventure, the felt life on a whaling ship, the humor and satire in the early chapters. These students tend to dislike the book's insistent metaphysical reach. For them the narrator's philosophizing not only deflects attention from the story but seems annoyingly wordy, preachy, and condescending. Other students find it exciting to follow the narrator from the real to the metaphysical, "when you can follow him, that is." As one said last summer, "I don't mind getting lost every so often, but you need *leisure* to read this book—you can't do it if you're working part-time." A third kind of response comes from a small minority, perhaps one or two in a class, who begin to feel an overwhelming awe for what Melville's mind could put together. More often than not, these students share Melville's enthusiastic alienation from American community norms. They admire the book's various rhetorical strategies for exploring and momentarily empowering the perceptive, independent mind. Still other students respond more intuitively if uneasily to the feelings of basic insecurity and powerlessness lying mute beneath the overflow of words. Finally, most students feel at least mildly curious about the historical contexts for *Moby-Dick*'s extravagant mental traveling.

Almost all these responses begin with a sense of confusion. Students feel upended by this text, and rightly so. Most want to enter a middle-class society from which Melville, with his lapsed-patrician angers and ironies, wants to escape or transcend. Melville's narrative plunges readers into a flow of disorientations that challenges and subverts almost everything a good American should believe in, from the worth of God, family, and profitable employment to the assumption that we have stable identities and coherent minds. The drive to prove one's cosmic importance and to test ultimate meanings, so central to *Moby-Dick*, strikes many students as unreal or, worse, egotistical. While some relish the subversiveness or creativity of the book's intellectual exuberance, others find the narrative self-indulgent, contradictory, evasive, and often tedious. Since their upper-middle-class professor ambivalently enlists on both sides, these tensions shape much of our discussion.

My first goal is to excite them about the book's surprises. Therefore I introduce it to all my classes in much the same way. At the end of the session before we start, I'll say something like this: "What's the first sentence of *Moby-Dick*?" Everybody says, " 'Call me Ishmael.' " "Wrong," I reply. "It's 'The pale Usher—threadbare in coat, heart, body, and brain; I see him now.'—I want you to find that sentence. Then I want you to think about why Melville would begin this story with a threadbare assistant schoolteacher whose translations of 'whale' get more and more far-fetched."

I'll also ask students to read the famous first paragraph of "Loomings" very slowly, several times, to see how odd it is. Why won't Ishmael tell us his name? What's his tone of voice? Do you like him? Look at the five or six reasons he gives for going to sea: how does he get from poverty and boredom to homicidal and suicidal tendencies, and why would he say everybody else feels the same way? Don't be afraid of your confusion, I'll say, and take the inflated language with a few grains of salt. It's a book that makes fun of itself all the time.

If someone contends next time that the first sentence really says, "In token of my admiration for his genius, this book is inscribed to Nathaniel Hawthorne," I'll know I've got at least one close reader who could spark more. Ordinarily about a third of the class will find something to say about the usher and the "poor devil of a Sub-Sub" (2) who piles up the extracts. Though I've asked people to read through chapter 23, "The Lee Shore," we may well spend the whole first session on the introductory pages and "Loomings."

Some students relish Ishmael's condescension toward both of his researchers, either because they like his arrogance or because it gives them the freedom to distrust him. Others seem perplexed that he sends the silly sub-sub to heaven while the more dignified if absurd usher gains nothing but mortality. Often the class and I get into a protracted fight over whether Ishmael mocks or values the usher. I say he likes the man: look at the balanced rhythms, the evocative phrasing, the wonderfully subtle ironies, the dead man's continuous presence in Ishmael's eye. They say threadbare means threadbare and anybody who thinks that much about dust has got to be crazy.

I usually lose that fight. It raises the level of attention, however, and helps to call authoritative answers into question. More alert to Melville's splash of detail, students also start to see how complicated Ishmael becomes when you try to unravel his words.

Eventually I or someone will suggest that Ishmael's presentations of the usher and the sub-sub reflect contradictory aspects of himself. His aggressive, ironic mind disengages from his own slavish desire to please. He delights in using the body's fate to puncture the mind's dreams, yet he loves to dream of immortality and spiritual fraternity. The mind-body tensions that surface here usually lead us into a discussion of Ishmael's feelings about Queequeg. I also spend a good deal of time on the usher's strange handkerchief, decorated with "all the gay flags of all the known nations of the world" (1). Why "mockingly embellished"? The usher doesn't love his "known nations" and the knowledge in his books; he loves to be reminded of their dust. How does that first piece of symbolism ironically frame Ahab's quest for whatever Moby Dick symbolizes? Students begin to realize that this book will be as much about hunting the mind as about hunting whales.

I haven't yet found a satisfactory way of organizing what happens next. I try to allot six sessions to *Moby-Dick* in undergraduate courses. Having fewer than six encourages wholesale skimming by instructor and students alike, while having more than six drives out too many other books. To stimulate active reading, I may ask students (if the class is under thirty) to come to the third or fourth class with a passage that pleases, annoys, or confuses them. That discussion can spring loose the riches of close reading and frequently highlights aspects of the narrative I'd never given much attention to. I'll also ask for a five- to six-page essay on one chapter or theme, again to stimulate detailed attentiveness. "The Doubloon" and the gams have been recent favorites, perhaps because they convey some sense of clarifying structure.

In class I usually linger on the first few pages, then spend the next two or three sessions in an ecstasy of passage hopping, chasing down the proliferating meanings and voices of one great paragraph after another, at the expense of more traditional concerns with symbolism, structure and character development. In fact I deliberately slight those concerns, because the book undermines the idea of form and character. I emphasize instead the pervasive opposition of truth telling to self-preservation and interpretive stability. In Father Mapple's sermon, "The Lee Shore," and various other instances of rhetorical intensity, I try to explicate the narrative's extravagant commitment to contrary postures of meaning.

Father Mapple, for example, passionately urges his Emersonian moral of being true to oneself rather than to society. Then he urges with equal zeal that we must strive to obey God and disobey ourselves. Almost in the same breath he says he knows little of God but "Thy rod." Yet he knows enough to declare that the "living God" has a "lifetime" like anybody else (50–51; ch. 9). Or what are we to make of Ishmael's 180° shift in chapter 26, where he rhapsodizes about solitary heroism and then rhapsodizes about democratic fraternity? The "spiritual terrors" of an enraged hero will compel Starbuck's "fall of valor in the soul." Yet the thought of Starbuck's upcoming fall leads

Ishmael to consider the "immaculate manliness" that "remains intact though all the outer character seems gone." Such manliness, which "bleeds with keenest anguish at the undraped spectacle of a valor-ruined man," has an intrinsic "dignity" that evokes Equality, Bunyan, Cervantes, Andrew Jackson, and finally God himself (104–05). The chapter's end seems to forget its middle. Why?

Lately I've been pushing harder and harder at Ishmael's contradictory narration. His voice both quickens and subverts Ahab's quest to discover and dominate meaning. Ahab's monomania clearly dehumanizes anyone who won't serve him as mirror en route to his destruction. Less clearly, Ishmael offers an evasive version of Ahab's interpretive narcissism. Yet Ishmael also explodes the need to be self-possessed. He contradicts himself with such aplomb, and so expansively, that he destabilizes any attempt to grasp him as a character with a fixed point of view.

How, I'll ask, can Ishmael assert so mordantly in "The Chapel" that "Faith, like a jackal, feeds among the tombs" and just a paragraph later talk himself into the spiritual immortality brought on by "a stove boat and stove body" (41)? Why, at the beginning of "Cetology," does he introduce his own monomania for whale classification with a short paragraph that moves from an evocative sense of being "unshored" to a blatant parody of scientific discourse (116)? Why, in the first chapter, does he say that the story of Narcissus is "the key to it all" (14) yet spend the rest of the chapter talking about slavery and fate?

Ultimately, I argue, his destabilizations give Ishmael a shapeshifter's oceanic voice while pushing landlubber readers considerably out of shape. Melville's story puts readers in a state of creative unsettlement, where answers become questions, quests mirror the quester, and identity itself becomes another form of slavery. "Is it I, God, or who, that lifts this arm?" Ahab cries in his most astonishing moment of revelation (445; ch. 132). If all of Ahab's egotistical drive has been decreed by the indifferent gods for their amusement, if the sun itself "is as an errand-boy in heaven," then to own any kind of character, integrity, or even consistent feelings makes one profoundly vulnerable. "The intense concentration of self in the middle of such a heartless immensity, my God! who can tell it?" Ishmael says of Pip in "The Castaway" (347). In that state of universal abandonment and paranoia, Ishmael's voice survives as a flux of spontaneous, arbitrary postures. Like a Cheshire cat, or the "masterless ocean" he describes in "Brit," his speaking takes on a playful, hostile, and devious fluidity, while Ahab's voice rigidifies into a doomed self-centering.

Let's say I was explicating Ishmael's double or triple pun on "Descartian vortices" at the end of "The Mast-Head" (140). I might start with the passage's portentous poke at Emerson. While some students remember the transparent eyeball at the beginning of Emerson's "Nature," it may be that nobody has ever heard of Descartes and pantheism or will admit they have, especially if the class is a sophomore introduction. So I'll briefly explain pantheism, then identify Descartes as the philosopher who said "Cogito, ergo sum," and the scientist who said that gravity results from the rotation of matter in vortices. So far, so good; the words go right into their notebooks, and I feel like an authority. But wait a minute: does "Descartian vortices" therefore refer to the danger of falling into the mind's self-referentiality or into the whirl of mortality brought on by physical matter?

Students seem relieved to discover that I can get as confused as they are about these things. But a deeper vortex is at hand. For several years I identified Descartes in a third way, as the mathematician who developed Cartesian coordinates (axis, vertex). That observation gave the allusion a third dimension, warning us about falling into the mind's analytic constructions. But recently a quiet student reclining in the back row raised his hand and—smashing my images of myself and my class—politely observed that my explication was nonsense. While Descartes did invent coordinate geometries as a way of resolving complex curvilinear motion, rectangular coordinates came along with Leibniz in the 1690s. Sure enough, volume 4 of the *Dictionary of Scientific Biography* says that Cartesian coordinates are misnamed, because Descartes never developed a fixed axial system. Moreover, various references that a chastened professor looked up in the same dictionary show how thoroughly eighteenth-century scientists had discredited Descartes's vortices, since the idea postulates the continuity of all matter without the possibility of vacuum or void.

So why would Melville use a discredited theory? Why would he use it at least two contrary ways at once? Why would he use it to evoke a void that invalidates the theory? And most important, did it really matter that I'd been giving them the wrong allusion all those years? Critics struggling with this allusion tend to cite a simpler use of the phrase in *Pierre* and give up. But if we push all the way, was either the author or the teacher doing much more than showing off? And what does that say about the mind's authority and integrity, when mind play continually bursts across the sky like a dazzle of wrong-way stars while one's body slips every moment toward mortality?

Moby-Dick incessantly forces me to admit that I move with my students from intellectual giddiness to the vortex of an almost visceral disorientation. That admission was hard to come by. In my first years of teaching this book I emphasized various theological explications of meaning, to the point that an intrepid student named Keith Davis finally burst out, "Hey, is this a course on religion or what?" I complemented God and anti-God with various neo-Freudian explications of motives: the search for mobile dicks; the fear of malicious fathers; the deeper search for mothering and milk versus the fear of heartless stepmothers who castrate, mutilate, and abandon their young. Now, while I'll never entirely back away from my own rage for explanation, I've come to think that much of what I took for emotional and metaphysical trauma is really rhetorical play, intended to dislodge us from self-centering.

One particularly fine graduate class, which spent well over an hour on the first paragraph of "Loomings," all but destroyed my sense of Ishmael as a repressed and tortured human being. Several students brilliantly argued that Ishmael isn't at all serious about himself here. The voice he presents is a series of conventional poses to induce and sabotage the reader's expectations. I'm still at sea about this. While my teaching continues to draw on the explanatory excitements from my early days, I feel a growing nervousness about how Melville toys with my need for authoritative coherence. Sometimes I quote Joseph Conrad's dismissal of *Moby-Dick* in a 1907 letter: "not a single sincere line in the whole 3 vols of it."[1] I think Melville would take it for a compliment.

A digression: once, while preparing chapter 76 for the next day's class, I felt at a loss to explain Ishmael's allusion to "the dread goddess's veil at Sais." In desperation I called Walter Bezanson, a friendly senior colleague and a well-known expert on Melville for many years. A chuckle came over the wires. At last he said, "It's all a mystery."

Eventually I retreat to structural issues. In the third or fourth class, for instance, I'll consider "The Town-Ho's Story" as what Richard Brodhead has called an "auxiliary heart" (13). (His fine *Hawthorne, Melville, and the Novel* is one of the depressingly few critical books on Melville that I regularly return to; another is Walter Herbert's Moby-Dick *and Calvinism*.) Since students generally see little relation between this tale and Ishmael's longer narrative, I'll end the previous class by asking them to come up with five or six connections next time. We usually open up a dozen or so: shared themes of predestination, malice, vengeance, authority; similar land-sea tensions in the fight between backwoodsman Radney and "ocean-born" Steelkilt; Moby Dick's "wondrous, inverted visitation" (208) as an agent of a just God rather than of ambiguous evil; the eruption here of a mutiny whose possibility is repressed in the main story. I'll also use the occasion to introduce Howard Vincent's idea that the Town-Ho's story may be the residue of what Melville had written before he encountered *King Lear* and Hawthorne (*Trying-Out* 46). Finally, Ishmael's narration here exposes his more covert mockery of his readers elsewhere. His lounging aristocratic listeners consistently deflect dramatic tension into an irrelevant concern for fixed labels. They wonder who Canallers are, they're fascinated by whether whales have Christian names. Their ridiculous responses try to appropriate a sea-ho story for their town-ho frames of reference.

Another way of stabilizing discussions of this unstable text is to consider the pros and cons of Robert Zoellner's thesis, in *The Salt-Sea Mastodon*, that Ahab's quest for dominance opposes a growing consciousness of ecological interdependence. "The Grand Armada" and "A Bower in the Arsacides" bring out the narrative's zest for constructive interweaving, balancing its equal zest for destructive unraveling. At first I didn't like Zoellner's thesis; it diminished Melville's "wicked book" to a Sierra Club tract. But one class pushed me a long way toward receptivity by pointing out all the positive images of nurturance, particularly of caring females, that creep in toward the end—not just the big ones in those two chapters but glancing, aching moments, such as Ishmael's account in "The Life-Buoy" of seal mothers who have lost their cubs (429). For those students "the devious-cruising Rachel" that picks up orphaned Ishmael in the epilogue completes a profound countermovement to male self-pity.

A related insight came from another class, again concerning the presence of female caring beyond male abilities to perceive it. An older student and mother, Louise Dutney, vigorously argued for a reinterpretation of Ishmael's dream in "The Counterpane." Though she could find no textual proof, she felt sure that the "nameless, unimaginable, silent form or phantom" (33) holding Ishmael's hand was really nothing more than his worried stepmother, who had come upstairs to sit quietly by his bedside. At first her idea seemed preposterous, very unlike her normally incisive and perceptive readings. "It just doesn't work," I said. "That's what my other professor said too," she replied. Prompted partly by competitiveness with my colleague and partly by respect for Louise, I began to explore the idea more seriously. Could it be that all the antimother passion I had taken at face value was part of the text's narcissistic male grandiosity?

In rethinking my teaching, I've gained some distance from my own participation in *Moby-Dick*'s alienated narcissism. I've also become aware of the Ahab and the Ishmael in my own classroom presence. My Ahab-like enthusiasm for discovering the text's "linked analogies" tends to transform each passage into what one student called "a mean springboard" for diving into the "hideous and intolerable allegory" that Ishmael mockingly entices us toward in "The Affidavit" (177). Yet Ahab's allegorical obsession reduces him from Promethean greatness to an alienated, mechanical demonism, much like Chillingworth's in *The Scarlet Letter*. Ahab himself comes to realize that his egotism may be an imposed role that stifles his feelings. Why is it, he asks, that "against all natural lovings and longings, I so keep pushing, and crowding, and jamming myself on all the time," when "my own proper, natural heart" craves human bonds, not destructive conquest (445; ch. 132)?

Similarly, Ishmael's enthusiasm for textual instability may mask a less grandiose but equally destructive self-avoidance, directed not at the whale but at himself as interpreter. Ishmael's mockery of his readers, or my pleasure in pulling the rug out from under my students' intellectual security, offers a pleasurably superior mode of disengaged hostility, even to one's own needs for security of mind. Do loss, need, and anger lurk there, as I still believe, or is he right to intimate that all meanings are simply self-projections to fill up a void? If the price of survival is the disappearance of his centered feelings and his own disappearance as a character, how can we respond beyond his terms?

I've come to trust my students a great deal here. Many of them have the clarity, common sense, and self-respect to withstand the text's deconstructive assaults, which I both indulge and criticize. My exposition of Ishmael's ability to destabilize himself and thus survive Ahab's quest once came to a dead stop when Lori Hartog said impatiently, "Ishmael survived because Queequeg couldn't write." More generally, students' annoyances can sometimes focus discussions beyond the all-points-loose interpretive ambience abetted by text and teacher.

Students can become extremely irked by *Moby-Dick*'s tenuous connection to female experience, its intimidating allusiveness, and its stop-again, start-again slog in the middle. The short chapters, the compressed contrary philosophies, and the quick alternation of levels and modes can alienate as well as intrigue. While it's useful to explore Melville's love-hate relation not just with readers but with the acts of reading and of making meaning, it's also useful to stand back from his evasive tussle with identity and maleness. "How come nobody in this book has two names?" one student asked incredulously. In stripping his characters down to their self-reliance, Melville robs them of the relations by which most of my students and I myself orient our lives.

Two particular challenges have stimulated exceptionally rich discussion. To many women the text's ambivalent and distanced use of female characters and imagery makes it boring. Sometimes feelings of real anger—and not just at the text—surface from beneath the boredom. At that point the text can become a safely neutral ground for discussing "male" and "female" as cultural constructs, each embedded with repressions, fears, desires. Leslie Fiedler and recent feminist social history of mid-nineteenth-century America have helped me here.

In talking about stereotypes of any kind, however, I've learned how silly it is to assume a generic response. When I was explicating what to me is one of Ishmael's grossest examples of sexism, his diatribe against painted women at the end of his meditation on whiteness, Mary Ellen Snook waved her hand dismissively. "That's just the conventional language of Melville's time," she said; "it's what he knew." For her, a premed student, Ishmael's scornful use of harlots seemed superficial compared to his parodic use of optics: "He was trying to get at science, not women." Throughout our discussions she delighted in Ishmael's play of mind: "He's building bricks on marshmallows." In another class, my careful and skittish introduction of homoerotic themes took an unexpected turn. As I was explicating Ishmael's sexual nervousness about Queequeg's entrance, Ezella Johnson interrupted to say that I had the perspective all wrong. She maintained with absolute conviction that Queequeg was really the homosexual, because he'd been out selling head in the streets.

Later in that series of discussions, Ezella raised what has become for me a basic challenge to the book's racial politics. Why is it that blacks never take on their bosses? Black folks' bodies serve white folks' spiritual needs, as visions of truth or comic relief. When Queequeg is overworked, he simply makes his coffin and lies in it. The coffin ultimately saves his white friend, not himself, like Sidney Poitier's self-sacrifice for Tony Curtis in *The Defiant Ones*. When the black cook, Fleece, is rudely shaken from sleep, he obediently humors Stubb by delivering a sermon to the sharks. While his matter carries a profound truth, that "all angel is not'ing more dan de shark well goberned," his manner is pure minstrel show (251; ch. 64). A third instance: Pip's spiritual drowning brings him to a deeper kind of slavish truth. The crazed black boy becomes a "conduit" for captain Ahab. Yet his craziness, while mirroring his master's, was brought on by Stubb's heartless abandonment. One student argued intriguingly that whites are truth-seeking while blacks are truth-telling. Yet what are the politics of a book whose authority figure is the only one to challenge authority?

At the vantage of 130 years, the blackness of Melville's "NO! in thunder" bears more than a touch of a white man's liberal presumption (Hayford and Parker 555). Claiming to act for all humanity, Ahab will challenge the authority of the grave itself rather than accept any limit to his own powers. In the process he refuses to acknowledge anyone else's distinct identity. While the narrative ambivalently frames Ahab's brooding centripetal manhood, the representative self that Ishmael assumes seems equally dehumanized and universalized, though in the opposite mode. Where Ahab blasts, Ishmael intellectualizes. Where Ahab attacks, Ishmael mocks. Where Ahab sulks into himself, Ishmael dreams of infinite narcissistic fraternity. But more than Ahab's rantings do, Ishmael's voice has the effect of magnifying mind and mystifying social conflict, as if he were Emerson's skeptical double.

In "The Poet" Emerson speaks of the essential "centrifugal tendency of a man," his need to "escape the custody of that body in which he is pent up, and of that jail-yard of individual relations in which he is enclosed" (234). The divided white man's self that Ahab and Ishmael enact presumes an alienation from one's body, one's groups, one's class, and one's world. Similarly, our classroom discussions will reflect that alienation, and the sexual and racial politics that follow hard upon it, unless we can find ways of acknowledging less universalized conflicts more directly. I try to do that primarily through student responses and secondarily by positioning the book in its time.

In practice, historical positioning frequently loses out to close reading, except as questions prompt me. Perhaps because the text evokes everything from burgeoning imperialism to a vanishing small-crafts industry, I've tended to explicate its jumble of genres less as connections to social history than as Melville's way of bringing to life the multiple stances inside himself. I do like to use his letters to Hawthorne, reprinted in the Norton edition, and I like to cite Hawthorne's 1856 summation as the finest single critical statement ever made about this complex man: "He can neither believe, nor be comfortable in his unbelief; and he is too honest and courageous not to try to do one or the other." I also like to read aloud Mrs. Hawthorne's letter describing Melville's "fluid consciousness" as he talked to Hawthorne.[2] Now that I'm starting to see the text's self-destructive self-referentiality from more social perspectives, I'll need to do more with social history, but I don't yet know what. The narrative absorbs all our time.

Recently a former student mentioned that what he remembered most about our sessions on *Moby-Dick* was how excited I got and how I'd say "page 347" as if it were an old friend. "Well," I said, "Pip's spiritual drowning is really crucial," before I realized that only the page number had stuck. He seemed amused that I could still dust off the page so easily. "You gay flags," he said cryptically.

I do cite key pages and phrases affectionately and repeatedly: "Who ain't a slave, tell me that?," "pasteboard masks," "boggy, soggy, squitchy picture," "insular Tahiti," "I look, you look, he looks." I use them as anchors or stepping stones to back off from instability toward pattern seeking and thematic mastery. Yet it's Melville's relish for unrest that really binds me to his text. Beyond and through his anarcho-aristocratic politics and the mirror tricks he loves to play, he immerses readers directly in the creative process.

One student concluded his course evaluation with the doubly underlined cry, "Where are the clear meanings?" *Moby-Dick* makes many readers feel inadequate, incoherent, annoyed. At least in my experience, however, only Emily Dickinson generates equally unpredictable, wild, and illuminating classroom responses. The two writers court fragmentation in ways that hit people right at the nerve and make some students say so. Like Emerson at his best, *Moby-Dick* also has the uncanny knack of wrenching out strange spontaneities. Its browbeating ventriloquism springs loose a rich variety of voices gone wooden with obedience to social codes. Alone among Melville's works, this book brings on the feeling of being creatively at odds with oneself as well as one's world.

Addendum

After drafting this essay, I sent a copy to Louise Dutney, the student whose ideas about the counterpane dream I first rejected then reconsidered. Her response corrects my mistaken sense that we'd thrashed out the issues in class that day and also brings out a "little lower layer" of her thinking. With her permission I quote the relevant portion of her letter:

You were correct to state in the class, when I commented on the Counterpane chapter, I couldn't come up with any textual proof and just felt instinctively that I was correct (I still do). You must remember that both you and —— had dismissed that notion out of hand. She had actually snickered, so naturally I never pursued it further with her. But you and I discussed the chapter a couple of times when I was in your office for class scheduling.

I then commented that Ishmael places the "fever dream," phantom hand experience in the same category with waking up with Queequeg's arm around him—an experience that he finds startling, but not completely unpleasant. Also, Ishmael calls his stepmother "the best and most conscientious of stepmothers." Granted, one can take this sarcastically, but I don't think so. For, even though he says that she was always beating him for something, he takes great pains to tell us that he was always in trouble, climbing up chimneys and such. Also, she couldn't be too terrifying because he goes down to throw himself on her mercy and she doesn't beat him or even yell at him.

After reviewing these observations when I got your note, I feel even stronger about the phantom hand/concerned stepmother connection. Ishmael/Melville(?) can't and probably doesn't want to recognize the innate kindness of the stepmother figure. All stepmothers are cruel, all mothers are overbearing, and this one can be no exception. Otherwise, the other images of male-bonding wouldn't hold up. After all, even the orphan-finding Rachel is "devious." Certainly, Melville could have used another adjective!

Finally, I think my interpretation holds up because in it, one can see the 19th century dilemma of the mind/body split. Ishmael's mind interferes, wants to distrust the stepmother, doesn't want to even consider her positively. But, the body's reactions are instinctive. Like an infant, his body recognizes the phantom touch as positive. For no matter how hard he wants to pull his hand away he actually falls asleep while in the phantom's clutches. What do you think?

NOTES

[1]See MacShane 464. Conrad's 15 January 1907 letter declines a request for him to write a preface to a new edition of *Moby-Dick*.

[2]See Hawthorne's much reprinted entry of 20 November 1856 in *The English Notebooks* (433). Mrs. Hawthorne's letter of 2 October 1851 to Elizabeth Peabody, her sister, is reprinted in Metcalf (106).

Less Erroneous Pictures of Whales: Open Structures in Teaching *Moby-Dick*

Robert F. Bergstrom

> . . . two and two there floated into my inmost soul,
> endless processions of the whale, and, midmost of
> them all, one grand hooded phantom, like a snow hill
> in the air.   (16; ch. 1)

The students had submitted their weekly journals. I had told them to finish reading *Moby-Dick* by today. One young woman wrote,

> what strikes me about this book is that Melville could have said what he had to say in no more than half of the length of *Moby-Dick*. I like adventure stories, and some of the chapters on the whale hunts were good. I liked the ending too (though I had a hard time getting that far). I think Melville took too long getting down to the story, and there's chapter after chapter where *nothing* happens.

A young man said in his journal, "I don't see why Melville makes such a big deal about Ahab trying to kill the whale. If some whale had bitten off my leg, I'd try to kill him too."

How was I to answer these students, either in notes on their journal pages or in my classroom presentation of the book? Of course, given several hours, I could have shown them in passionate detail the glories and depths of this unique masterpiece. I first read *Moby-Dick* in high school and was captivated by its language, its sound. By the time I came to write my dissertation, the book had ceased to be merely an interest or a pleasure; it had become an obsession. When I began my college teaching career, I felt fully qualified to answer my students' questions and comments.

It didn't take me long to realize how ill-prepared I was. With few exceptions, the students were not haunted, as I was, by Ishmael's "hooded phantom." I tried to tell them of the book's style, its structure, its profundity. They were polite but unmoved. It became clear that the only students who profited by my talking were those few who already had a vague sense of what I would say. I was frustrated and angry. Ultimately, in my slow way, I came to understand that my task in teaching *Moby-Dick* was not simply to get the students to read this "classic" and answer questions about it. No, the real challenge was to encourage students who were put off rather than intrigued by the book's mysteries to explore the dangerous intellectual and emotional terrain of Melville's "white world." And so I came to what I intend to share here: not so much a method of teaching *Moby-Dick* (I have used several) as a philosophy.

I begin with a paradox. On the one hand, *Moby-Dick* works its deepest magic by indirection and nuance. Moreover, it is an open-ended narrative, a doubloon that mirrors to the reader his or her own fears, preoccupations, and biases. To stand before a class of undergraduates and tell them what the book "means," then, is to do violence to Melville's fictional technique as well as to his skeptical, dialectical thinking. On the other hand, the book is so labyrinthine that it would be irresponsible to abandon one's students to its depths, like Pip, and expect them to emerge whole. *Moby-Dick* cannot be well understood without some sense of the immediate and remote contexts within which it was written. More important, my reading in developmentalist epistemology (particularly that of Piaget) indicates that many students will come to the book unprepared to make the higher-order integrations of abstract data that *Moby-Dick* demands. For example, a teacher can show students the similarity among the mat-maker image, the God whose foot Pip sees on the treadle of the loom, and Ishmael's weaver God (chs. 47, 93). Even so, many will fail to see that this is not merely a sequence of repeated images. The reader has to hold in mind Ishmael's image of personal control over destiny, place it in the context of the remote power of Pip's vision, and then combine both of them with the mechanical, naturalistic image of the weaver God. Without performing this complicated mental task, the reader cannot fully understand any of the three images. Given a book replete with such difficulties, a teacher must provide ordered guidance if the students' exploration of Ishmael's narrative is to yield anything but frustration and boredom. But how can one offer students intelligent and informed structure in the classroom without imposing on them a rigid interpretative stance that not only runs counter to Melville's method but likely will bewilder most students?

The matter of contexts is more easily talked about than taught. In some ways forty years ahead of his time when he wrote *Moby-Dick*, Melville was still a product of his nation and his era. There is so much in the book (by influence or likeness) of the Puritans, Franklin, Emerson, Thoreau, Hawthorne, and Whitman that these writers provide an indispensable guide to interpretation. As a result, I either teach *Moby-Dick* near the end of a survey or spread the reading out over the course of the semester. Using the latter method I will, for example, pair Father Mapple with the Puritans, Ahab with Thoreau, "The Masthead" with Emerson, and "The Try-Works" with Hawthorne. Biographical information about Melville (along with the letters he wrote while working on *Moby-Dick*) I intersperse with our discussion of Ishmael and Ahab so as to encourage the students to discover similarities between the author and those two rather different characters.

The ordering of the classroom presentation is, of course, considerably more complicated. I see *Moby-Dick* as a book composed of one triad on the narrative level and another on the intellectual level. The first triad, Ishmael-whale-Ahab, involves an examination of two seekers who use the whale as the focal point of their quests. Ishmael, both within the narrative and more extensively through his storytelling, seeks to establish, at least tentatively, a method for creating meaning in a world of flux and mystery. Ahab seeks truth itself through the anticipated act of impaling his dismemberer. The second triad, God-nature-humanity, constitutes the major intellectual focus of the book. It represents a complex set of relations through which each of the major characters manifests his view of the world, and it thereby becomes both the energizing force and the object of the book's central quest. On both levels, I see Ishmael's voice as crucial. The narrative is more than a reflection on his voyage with Ahab; it is an attempt to manufacture meaning from violence and chaos, from the monomania of Ahab and the incomprehensibility of the whale.

On the basis of this interpretation, I divide the study of the book into four sections: Ishmael (chs. 1–23), Ahab (chs. 24–54), cetology (ch. 55–105), and finale (ch. 106–epilogue). I see some advantage in dealing with at least the first two sections as the students read rather than waiting until they've finished the book. My task in the first section is to encourage the students to understand Ishmael's condition at the book's beginning, to climb inside his skin and see him much as Conrad's Marlow wishes his auditors to do. Since I want the students to share Ishmael's experiences, I have them share their experience of him by working in groups to produce a profile of Ishmael's mood and outlook, usually from chapters 2 and 3. After presenting the results of this exploration, the students go back to "Loomings" and compare its tone with that of the two chapters that follow it. Such a comparison helps the students discover that the Ishmael who tells the story is not quite the same as the man who lived it, that a period of time has passed between the action and the telling. ("The Town-Ho's Story" is an important chapter for the same purpose.)

Such a concentration on the first few chapters ought to give students the background they need to discuss the rest of my first section. The matters emphasized in discussion are likely to be those the teacher deems critical—Queequeg, the Ishmael-Queequeg relation, Father Mapple, the choice of the *Pequod*, and Bulkington offer themselves. Two larger issues, however, seem to me important at this stage. First, it is vital, whatever focus the teacher brings to the discussion, that the students build on and apply to new scenes or ideas the knowledge they've constructed about Ishmael. I myself follow Melville's lead in these early chapters and point everything toward Ishmael's perceptions, Ishmael's fears, Ishmael's value system. Second, in this early stage of discussion a teacher should help the students confront the style and language of the book. An often overlooked way of accomplishing this end is to read aloud and to have the students do so. Students who read to one another portions of the first three chapters will not only begin to overcome the strangeness of Melville's stylistic mannerisms but also learn more about Ishmael himself than a lecture on his narrative method could possibly convey. Indeed, throughout the study of the book, there are great advantages to having the class pronounce and hear Melville's language. For example, a teacher with a good voice could read part of Mapple's sermon and then ask how Ishmael could hear such an oration, only to form an alliance with a heathen cannibal and help him worship Yojo.

The next section of the book (chs. 24–54) concentrates on Ahab, with two significant irruptions of Ishmael in his own right. These chapters give the reader Ahab's first appearance on deck, the announcement of the hunt and the crew's reaction, Ishmael's analysis of Ahab's quest (and of his own), the first lowering and the appearance of Fedallah, and the spirit spout. The section ends with an elegant older Ishmael reinforcing his role of storyteller and interpreter of Moby Dick in "The Town-Ho's Story." As with our discussion of Ishmael, my aim in this section is to help the students see the world as Ahab sees it, always keeping in mind Ishmael's controlling voice. Again the possibilities of focus are numerous, and not all can be explored. One might, for example, wish to highlight Melville's insistence on the power of a ship's captain, so clearly stated before Ahab even appears. In groups, students can role-play captain and crew, feeling the deference (grudging or not) that a captain demanded. Such an activity allows the class to probe Ishmael's immediate and long-range response to his captain, as well as to understand his analysis of Ahab's use and misuse of power. More important, given the other evidence we have about Ahab, his assumption of unchallenged authority helps explain his fury at his dismemberment, not to mention his extraordinary confrontation with his first mate on the quarterdeck.

Whatever approach one uses, it is important that the students neither distance themselves too greatly from Ahab nor take him too lightly. The dangers of the latter position are obvious, those of the former more subtle. Unless the students can feel the torments of the man, can sense his greatness of mind and spirit, the novel will seem to them no more than a drawn-out exercise in bombast (and quite rightly). I find two measures useful in avoiding this result. First, I introduce students at this point to Melville's letters (available in the Norton Critical Edition), particularly those to Hawthorne. These letters not only provide valuable insights into the novel but also demonstrate to what extent Ahab reflects one side of Melville's personality. Second, it is important that the students recognize how seriously Ishmael takes Ahab (one reason why they must take *Ishmael* seriously). I have the students work out Ahab's motivation as well as the significance of the whale's whiteness without access to the book. Even if they have read "Moby Dick" and "The Whiteness of the Whale," such an exercise is not a mere test of memory, and it serves to impress on them the cosmic nature of Ahab's quest for vengeance.

The cetology section of the book (chs. 55–105) is without doubt the most difficult to deal with in the classroom. Not only are the convolutions of Ishmael's intellectual exploration staggering in their complexity, but most new readers don't like this section. How many of us have had the frustrating experience of being told by our more outspoken students that the whaling chapters are boring and irrelevant to the book's progress and outcome? Still, we should keep in mind that many professional critics with no stake in enhancing Melville's reputation have said much the same thing.

Most students are willing to acknowledge, I think, that the information about whales and whaling contributes to our understanding of the skill and danger involved in whaling as well as of the whale's magnificence. They will complain, nonetheless, that Melville has overdone a good thing. The teacher's task, as I see it, is to have them discover Ishmael's exploration of the God-nature-humanity triad in these chapters. I say "discover" quite deliberately, for unless students first see for themselves that Ishmael uses whaling as an extended image of human life, they will never accept a teacher's assertion that such is the case.

Perhaps the easiest way to get students thinking about the cetology chapters is to concentrate briefly on the natural part of the triad, here represented chiefly by the whale. I intend for them to find out that their likely impression of the purpose of this section is not accurate. For example, I ask the students to look in groups at chapters about whales (55–56, 68, 70, 74–76, 79, 80, 85, 86, 102, 103–05). If they boil down each chapter to what can and cannot be known about whales and if their joint results are recorded on a chalkboard, they will discover that the list of unknowables at least equals that of what can be known. Having assumed that they were drowning in esoteric facts about the whale, they are likely to be surprised and puzzled, thus allowing the teacher to help them apply their insight to important matters of the book. At the center of the book, at the end point of Ahab's quest, lies a mystery, no less a phantom than is the spirit spout and one often teasingly identified with the Deity. What does this fact say not only about Ahab and Ishmael but about human life itself, since, as we have been told, the whale lives "among the unspeakable foundations, ribs, and very pelvis of the world" (118; ch. 32)?

Armed with the knowledge that Ishmael does more than supply anatomical descriptions of whales in chapters 55–105, the students may be ready to confront the manifold and ambiguous purposes of this section. A teacher can push them in that direction quite simply. I assign each student the task of discovering at least one thing in these chapters that has to do with matters beyond whales and whaling. What they find and share with the rest of the class will overlap considerably, but the important thing is that they see, however vaguely, that these chapters contain a pattern of thinking, not just facts. Once students grasp this point, they can think systematically about crucial passages in the section. I have no qualms about structuring their exploration of such passages once I am sure that they are themselves convinced that there is something real to look for.

That structuring, however, presents me with my greatest critical problem as a teacher of *Moby-Dick*. If I cheat on my system a little and include "The Masthead," "The Mat-Maker," and "The Hyena," I find that before chapter 106 Ishmael has explored a wide range of responses to the world he and Ahab share and has attained insights that allow him to see that world for what it is without risking a descent into Ahab's madness. Such an interpretation, however, demands a subtle demonstration because Ishmael's thinking is not conveniently organized in climactic fashion. Rather, it is scattered and at times contradictory, growing organically from whatever aspect of the narrative or of whaling he happens to be discussing. (For example, "The Lee Shore" is contradicted by "A Squeeze of the Hand." Does the latter suspersede the former? Or, as I believe, is each chapter less of a definitive statement than it appears?)

Faced with the symbolic complexity of Ishmael's moral quest, I am tempted to chart a course for my students through the cetology section. But having worked diligently to help them understand the book on their own, I would be foolish at this point to lecture on ultimate meanings. What I do, instead, is provide the students with a list of passages from my cetology section and ask them to draw a new profile of Ishmael, working through the contradictions as best they can. In order to focus the discussion, I ask them always to compare what Ishmael says with what they think Ahab would say on the same issue. In this way, whether they arrive at an Ishmael close to mine or not, they will at least see how Ishmael develops his worldview in the face of the one that prompted the narrative in the first place—Ahab's.

Teacher and students can now turn to the final section of the book with something of a head start, since that section focuses directly on Ahab and the results of his approach to the world and its evil. If the classroom work on the book has gone relatively well so far, this section will not demand teaching so much as energy and sensitivity on the part of the class. The discussion of this section ought to balance what was likely a rather abstract approach to the previous one. These chapters deal directly with relations between humans (or with the absence of such relations). It is here that essential choices are made between life and death, which may account for the seemingly irrelevant chapter on Queequeg's "death."

Despite the high drama of some later chapters, their focus on basic humanity should remind the students of Melville's warning against viewing the book as a "hideous and intolerable allegory" (177; ch. 45). Ahab and his fellow whalers may in some ways be larger than life, but they are also renegades and castaways who are closer to the reader than are the heroes and villains of ancient tales. The students will see clearly Ahab's "fatal pride" (425; ch. 124), so reminiscent of Milton's Satan; but they should also look closely at his condition before the final chase—an isolated man among "Isolatoes" (108; ch. 27) and a lonely and finally helpless human being whose vision of evil has become too narrow and too intense. In this connection, I have asked students what arguments they might make to persuade Ahab to abandon his pursuit of the whale, urging them to take into account their response to his pitiful rejection of Starbuck and Pip.

In short, we should not let Melville's wisdom in humanizing the last section of *Moby-Dick* escape us or our students, for the direction in which he moves the book as it nears its climax will help the students answer intelligently two questions that they will very much want answered—why does Ahab die, and why does Ishmael live? Many students will, without careful consideration, interpret the ending of *Moby-Dick* as the early critics of this century did: Ahab dies because he is a blasphemer or a prideful rebel; Ishmael lives because he is a right-thinker who accepts the world as it is ordained by Providence. By stressing the human rather than the cosmic elements of the narrative, as I think Melville intends, I consciously encourage students to question such notions. Even if they leave our discussion of the book with the opinion that moral justice has been done at the end, I want students to ponder the human cost of the *Pequod*'s sinking—the death of an innocent like Pip, the drowning of others who did not consciously follow Ahab, the grief of families. I want them, too, to ask what force it is that saves Ishmael and how it differs from the power Ahab believes rules the world.

After its blood and turmoil, *Moby-Dick* ends peacefully. Ahab has followed Fedallah to the only rest he has known for a great while. An orphaned Ishmael is picked up by an anxious parent searching for another lost child. But careful readers remember Melville's warnings—the peace is to a degree illusory. We are left with the emotions of terror and pity, but more those of *King Lear* than of *Oedipus*, since the novel shares the awful and ironic ambiguity of Shakespeare's play. Melville's is a world that is beautiful and dangerous, appalling and gentle; a world in which noble and base elements mix freely, not just among humans but within them; a world where the great and powerful may do evil or go mad and where the weak may shine as does the sun, if only briefly. It is that world that I want my students to see, whatever their ultimate interpretation of *Moby-Dick* might be.

One may, I suppose, simply tell students who have read *Moby-Dick* that it is rich in ambiguity, but I don't think that approach will do them much good. If I expect my students to deal with the mysteries and convolutions of *Moby-Dick* as intelligent readers, I must open for them the opportunity to feel the difficulties and work through them. I try, slowly at first, to get them to say what they know about what they've read, making sure that they have the opportunity to hear what their peers think. Then I ask them to build on that knowledge, moving from what they do understand to what they do not and applying past insights to current uncertainties. Ultimately, each student will reach a point at which a mystery or ambiguity in the book will not resolve itself in the light of previous thinking. Those of us who have been haunted by *Moby-Dick* have all come to just such places. My way of helping students over these blocks is to keep bringing our exploration and discussion back to the fact that, Shakespearean grandeur aside, *Moby-Dick* is a narrative written by a decent man looking for a satisfying course through a world that is sometimes indecent and often incomprehensible. Even my most ingenuous students know of such a world, and they can understand and sympathize with Ishmael's efforts, even when he isn't as clear and straightforward as they might like.

I don't expect undergraduates reading *Moby-Dick* for the first time to understand it fully, but then Melville expected no such thing of his readers. What did anger him was their biased refusal at times to grant the possible validity of what he had to say. I think, at least, that we can help our students become the kind of "thought-divers" (Davis and Gilman 79) that Melville sought so earnestly all his life.

"Trying All Things": *Moby-Dick* in Pieces

Christopher W. Sten

Teaching *Moby-Dick* can be a daunting task. Melville's book is a famous masterpiece, a perennial candidate for the Great American Novel, a weighty epic of extraordinary verbal difficulty. Those who would attempt to teach it need brains, to be sure, but even more they need backbone, in the proportion that characterizes the whale. For to be an effective teacher of the book one needs the fortitude to develop a wide range of talents. At the least, one must try to become almost everything Ishmael is: epic poet, whaling expert, biblical scholar, stage director, narrator, performer, humorist, truth seeker, and (in rare moments) truth teller. But one should also work to serve one's students as literary historian, Shakespearean, Americanist, philologist, and philosopher, as well as Socratic insinuator, provoker, moderator, devil's advocate. Harder still, one needs to perform all these roles with Ishmael's unobtrusive artistry, and all in less time than it takes to read the book: in each of my advanced undergraduate courses—The Nineteenth-Century American Novel and American Romanticism—I can usually devote just two and a half weeks to Melville's novel, or five seventy-five-minute class periods. Add to these difficulties the fact that, like the whale itself, Melville's novel has a reputation for eluding, if not actually punishing, those who attempt to capture it, and the prospect for success seems doleful indeed. When faced with the opportunity to teach *Moby-Dick*, one does well, therefore, to follow the lead of Ishmael himself when he says, "I try all things; I achieve what I can" (291; ch. 79). More than anything else, it is the attitude implied in this statement—the mixture of daring and sanity typical of Melville's narrator—that I try to teach when I teach *Moby-Dick*.

Over the past ten years or so I have developed various procedures for trying to ensure comprehensive treatment of *Moby-Dick*, knowing well that every reader lacks the "Time, Strength, Cash, and Patience" necessary to grasp the book in its entirety (128; ch. 32). My principal strategy has been to divide and conquer, as Ishmael does when he anatomizes the whale. I have students read the novel in five approximately equal sections of ninety to one hundred pages each, fixing the exact boundaries between them at those threshold points where Melville shifts from one major subject or cluster of subjects to another. In my formulation, the first section consists of "Loomings" through "The Lee Shore" (chs. 1–23), the land-based portion centering on themes of preparation for embarking on the *Pequod*'s hunt. The second segment begins with "The Advocate," wherein Ishmael acts as an epic poet, celebrating the heroism of his fellow whalers while conveying something of the fearsome reputation of Ahab's great antagonist, the whale; it ends with "The Mat-Maker" (ch. 47), where the rude appearance of the first whale encountered on this voyage suddenly interrupts Ishmael's marvelous weaving of a theory on the connectedness of fate, free will, and chance. Part three, in turn, centers on whaling practices—the pursuit, killing, and securing of the beast—starting with "The First Lowering" and concluding with Ishmael's reflections on the sperm whale's head, as its carcass hangs from the ship, in "The Battering Ram" (ch. 76). The fourth section emphasizes the various consequences of hunting and capturing the whale—the rewards and the dangers of the enterprise—and provides several warnings as to the madness of Ahab's quest; it runs from "The Great Heidelberg Tun" to "The Decanter" (ch. 101) and as a unit focuses also on the romance themes of containment, transformation, and deliverance. The final part, while it continues the themes of romance, develops even more prominently the themes of tragedy; it opens with Ishmael undergoing a trial inside a whale (a whale skeleton) in "A Bower in the Arsacides" and ends with the epilogue, where he alone is found to have escaped the fury of the great white whale.

On the first day of class, there are, besides the land-based chapters, several preliminaries to discuss: Melville's career before *Moby-Dick*, his dedication of the book to Hawthorne, the etymologies and the extracts, the variety of forms he used in composing the book. Concerning each of these subjects, I emphasize the extraordinary ambition of Melville's undertaking. Virtually everything Melville did in this book was aimed at producing what he termed "a mighty book" (379; ch. 104); most of what I do, therefore, is aimed at disclosing what makes it a book of this kind. I point out that Melville was at the peak of his powers—buoyed by personal happiness at his growing family; by the sureness of his previous novels, *Redburn* and *White-Jacket*; by the liberating experience of reading Shakespeare deeply for the first time; and by his discovery of the American example of the older Hawthorne. Next we talk about the reasons one writer would dedicate his work to another, and then we look at Melville's famous review of Hawthorne's *Mosses from an Old Manse* (reprinted in the Norton Critical Edition of *Moby-Dick*) for clues as to why Melville wanted his readers to think of Hawthorne and himself as kindred spirits. I read aloud the passages on the "power of blackness" and original sin, on the remarkable "short, quick probings at the very axis of reality" that Melville found characteristic of Shakespeare and Hawthorne, and on the "great Art of Telling the Truth"—all of which help to define Melville's romanticism, his profound concern with the essence as distinct from the surface of things, with the metaphysical dimension of existence as distinct from the physical, with the truth to be apprehended through insight rather than through eyesight (Hayford and Parker 540–42).

When I talk about the etymologies and the extracts, I have to reveal that *Moby-Dick* is written from the point of view of a survivor of a catastrophe. This much must be said at the start to account for the edgy, morbid tone of the opening chapters and to make the point that Ishmael is, at the time he begins to write *Moby-Dick*, a broken, searching, strangely modern figure, like Tiresias in Eliot's *The Waste Land* who captures Ishmael's state of mind when he says, "These fragments I have shored against my ruins." As one of my students has argued in a recent dissertation, Ishmael's extraordinary collection of extracts reveals his obsession with the beast of destruction, the cause of his ruin, at the same time it reveals, by its lack of order or comment, Ishmael's numbness and inability to make sense of what he has lived through (Reno). Those extracts on the whale, coming as they do from other works of literature, are also like the pieces of a fertility god that are scattered across the land to restore it to life in the spring; they contain within them the seeds of the hero's resurrection, as the writings of the past often do. I plant this idea early because it provides a chance to propose the belief, common among romantic writers, in the health-restoring power of art—a chief motive behind Ishmael's writing of *Moby-Dick*. And it helps to lay the groundwork necessary to suggest parallels later between Melville's story of the wounded Ahab and the myth of the impotent Fisher King, with its underlying assumption that the "waste" and the restoration of the land depend on the leader's attitude toward the natural realm, on the purity of his motive for attempting to capture the fish (a universal symbol of fertility) whose fate is mysteriously connected with the health of the land and of the people who inhabit it.

The last of the preliminaries I take up is form. I begin with the assertion that *Moby-Dick* is written in the tradition of the epic, particularly the quest epic like the *Odyssey*, but modernized and Americanized—its heroes not the gods (and goddesses) and godlike nobles of Homer's poem but rough-hewn democratic "*Isolatoes*" (108; ch. 27), its subject not the wars between rival peoples and the protracted return of a Greek prince but the big business of American whaling during the 1840s and the vengeful quest of a Nantucket captain. I point out the epic nature of the book early in the discussions because students need to know something of *Moby-Dick*'s generic context if they are to understand Melville's fundamental strategy and appreciate his adaptation of traditional literary form for his own purposes—not just the early folk epic but other forms, too. Like his contemporaries, Whitman and Thoreau, Melville experimented with established forms of writing, reshaping them as his imagination and his sense of the historical moment dictated. To give the class some advance warning of the medley of forms to be encountered later in the book, I mention that *Moby-Dick* incorporates elements of comedy and tragedy; of history, satire, anatomy, and autobiography; of drama, poetry, sermon, novel, and romance; and of the age-old fish story, too—the tale of the really big one that got away. To round out this part of the discussion I offer my own definition of the composite form of *Moby-Dick*. Using terms informed chiefly by Northrop Frye, I call it a "tragic epic romance with a comic introduction and epilogue—or a comic 'frame.'"

When I turn to the patterns of action, the fundamental themes and motifs of the first assignment, I begin by asking my students what they have found to be the underlying values or attitudes Melville has attached to the land and the sea respectively in the first twenty-three chapters. Using the blackboard, I try to get the class to offer as many qualities or pairs of contrasting qualities as they can, under the basic dichotomy of land and sea. This exercise helps to break the ice, providing a simple format whereby even shy students can participate; it quickly makes consideration of the book a collective enterprise; and it gives all members of the class an early chance to see how their level of reading and command of the book measures up to those of their peers. After this recital of impressions, I make my own additions to the list or simply summarize, perhaps while highlighting my own favorite notions. At the same time, I make sure there has been adequate recognition of Ishmael's motives in turning to the sea: his quest for health, as seen in his attempt to conquer his suicidal "hypos"; his craving for self-knowledge, as seen in his narcissistic fascination with water, a variation of Emerson's idea that one can best know oneself by studying nature; his desire to know the meaning of the world, or a large part of it, as seen when he tells Captain Peleg, "I want to see what whaling is. I want to see the world" (69; ch. 16). And then I touch on the themes of preparation, particularly concerning Ishmael: the initiation he goes through, under Queequeg's tutelage, as he moves back in consciousness and in time to the primitivism of the whalemen; the stripping away of his conventional, citified ways, as he gets down to the essential human of independent mind and natural feeling (as Thoreau and Whitman would do at the beginning of *Walden* and "Song of Myself") before the *Pequod*'s voyage; the transvaluation of values he undergoes, as he exchanges his Victorian prudery for the tolerance and common sense of the man of nature ("Better sleep with a sober cannibal than a drunken Christian," he admits—to cite but one example—after his first night with Queequeg [31; ch. 3]); the discovery of the Polynesian's love and regard that starts him on the way to healing.

For these matters, I pay close attention to "Loomings" and "The Lee Shore," the latter for its brief portrait of the phantom Bulkington, an alter ego of Ishmael's and the epitome in *Moby-Dick* of the romantic quester. But I also look, briefly, at several other chapters in this first assignment (3–5, 10–13, and 17–18—all treating Ishmael's growing friendship with Queequeg) to point out the comic qualities of Melville's book: the wordplay and prattle, Ishmael's nosiness and alarmism, his pratfalls and comeuppances, even his mock marriage with his future shipmate. I do this to suggest that Melville's mind, like those of his mentors, Hawthorne and Shakespeare, was not unvaryingly tragic in outlook, that it was whole, even in this darkening middle phase of his career. And then I look carefully at the three chapters

(7–9) centering on the Whaleman's Chapel in New Bedford, for three reasons: first, because they provide the book's only extended development of its biblical themes—disobedience and trial, obedience and deliverance; second, because they offer some schooling in the symbolic method of the book, through Ishmael's musing on the meanings, for example, of the memorial tablets on the walls and of the actions of Father Mapple; and third, because Mapple's sermon, with its "two-stranded lesson," offers an important framework for judging Ahab's vengeful hunt and an apt formulation of Ishmael's mission as artist when he comes back from the dead, namely, to "preach the Truth to the face of Falsehood" (45–50).

With luck and some fast talking, there is time at the end of the first day to make a few remarks about the romance structure of *Moby-Dick* and about Ishmael as an archetypal quester. Using Frye's *The Secular Scripture* and Joseph Campbell's *The Hero with a Thousand Faces* as background, I offer a preliminary formulation of the idea that Ishmael, in going to sea, recapitulates the fundamental story of every successful hero of myth, folklore, and romance. He leaves the familiar waking world of daily affairs and, with the help of a friendly guide or "double," moves through an "underworld" of dreams and nightmares, of adversity and torment—as Aeneas and Dante, for instance, had before him. This underworld is known as "the belly of the whale," in Campbell's terminology (90)—the place of trial, where the hero experiences imprisonment and violence and undergoes a breakup, even a loss, of his old identity, only to discover his deeper, truer identity at the nadir of his adventure, as Ishmael does much later in chapter 94, "A Squeeze of the Hand." Having discovered that he is miraculously free to become what he wills and that he is capable of love, he comes back, after facing the equivalent of the Beast of Apocalypse, with the knowledge of death and of his own vitality that makes him a true hero—a man with the inchoate wisdom that can restore health to the dying nation that does not even know it awaits his return.

On the second day, I shift from talking about *Moby-Dick* as a romance to talking about it as an epic. Ishmael himself signals such a change when, in the first chapter of this section, "The Advocate," and in the next seven chapters, he takes on the role of an unconventional epic singer who celebrates the "unpoetical" subject of whaling and the uncommon heroism of the hunters of whales (98). Again I use the board to open up class discussion. This time we work up a definition of the epic, or a list of its characteristics; simultaneously we measure the ways in which *Moby-Dick* does and does not fit the form—or ways in which Melville has extended or altered it. This is a hard question for discussion, especially for nonmajors, because it requires some prior knowledge of the form—knowledge of *Paradise Lost*, for instance. But no student should feel stymied once the definition of "epic" is loosened up to include popular novels or movies in the genre, such as *Gone with the Wind, The Godfather*, or *Star Wars*. To help ensure a comprehensive definition, I ask the class to consider all the major building blocks of any narrative—character, plot, setting, theme, style, scene, and point of view.

In the second segment, chapters 24–47, the reader is also given Ahab's and Ishmael's contrasting views of the whale, the two principal ones among many in the book. These in turn provide two fundamentally different ways of seeing, two conflicting sets of attitudes about the world; as such they are the book's two major instances of the related themes—to be found in virtually every work of fiction Melville wrote after *Moby-Dick*—of blindness and vision. During the rest of the second day, then, I begin to take up the tricky epistemological subject of the symbolism of the whale, the ever fascinating and elusive matter of what Moby Dick represents. When we consider Ahab's view of the whale, we look first at the famous "pasteboard masks" speech in "The Quarter-Deck" (ch. 36) and then at several paragraphs in "Moby Dick" that culminate in the idea that "crazy Ahab" has *projected* "all evil" onto the whale's white hump (159–60; ch. 41). By implication, Melville presents Ahab's way of seeing as a warning against certain dangers inherent in the romantic use of the imagination as a "lamp," an idea outlined in M. H. Abrams's *The Mirror and the Lamp*. Here I query the class about what lies behind the psychological mechanism of projection and about the sources of Ahab's rage at the whale, noting its parallel with the "unjust wound" found in the work of Hemingway, the seemingly arbitrary violence that destroys one's potency or makes one aware of the powerlessness that is the common lot. At some point, most students seem to benefit from a discussion of what ails Ahab. His affliction, after all, is the primum mobile of the whole bloody hunt; for a reader who at the so-called gut level is unsure about Ahab's motives, most of the book will not make much sense.

In what remains of the second period, I at least begin to talk about Ishmael's more complicated view of the whale, as presented in the tour de force, "The Whiteness of the Whale" (ch. 42), though inevitably most of what I want to say has to wait until the next meeting. This subject is the most subtle and, for me, the most haunting of Melville's book. I outline Ishmael's exploration of his terror at the whale's whiteness virtually paragraph by paragraph, and then I read aloud the last several paragraphs centering on the Vermont colt's "instinct of the knowledge of the demonism of the world" (169), Melville's equivalent of what Kant in *Critique of Pure Reason* called "transcendental" or a priori knowledge, a cornerstone of romantic thinking. Here Ishmael comes closer than ever to the position that Moby Dick is inherently evil and can intuitively be known to be such. However, he does not rest on that point as a certainty. Instead, he admits that "not yet have we solved the incantation of this whiteness" and in effect cancels out the Kantian stance by voicing his suspicion that the meaning of the whiteness of the whale, and by extension the meaning of all nature, is subjective and relative—in itself, nothing more than "a colorless, all-color of atheism from which we shrink" (169). Thus in the end, I find it necessary to shift emphasis from the romantic qualities of Ishmael's investigation into the power of whiteness to its prophetically modern qualities. For in wondering whether all significance that one sees in the world is projected onto it by the consciousness of the perceiver, as a movie projector casts an image on a white screen, Ishmael comes to the verge of the existentialist notion that the world has existence but not necessarily essence.

What is most remarkable about Ishmael's rendering of this position is that to the end it remains for him a question. He never actually reaches the existentialist position; he never embraces it as an absolute certainty. In "The Whitness of the Whale," as in every other chapter in which he offers lessons on the whale's anatomy—"The Blanket" (ch. 68) and "The Fountain" (ch. 85) are particularly good (and funny) examples in later sections—Ishmael remains suspicious of absolutes. More than any other character in the book, he is comfortable with hypotheses as the bases of all thinking and living. Unlike the absolutist Ahab, Ishmael can make and withhold judgments at the same time; unlike Ahab, the man of certainty, he knows that the whale, like the world of which it is a part, forever defies human attempts to make sense of it in definitive terms, that it will forever elude humanity's grasp. That, finally, is what Ishmael finds so appalling about the whale's whiteness: like everything else, it is beyond our knowing.

During the third period, once I finish assessing Ishmael's view of the whale, I try to get my students to do more thinking on their own about the dominant images and motifs, the underlying themes and structures of the book. I ask them to turn to the table of contents for chapters 48–76 and, using the chapter titles as a guide, to look for major recurring ideas and groupings of chapters in this section. By now they should be able to develop their own sense of the book's important patterns, but if they need prompting, I adopt a functionalist approach as a means of leading the class in discussion, asking them for explanations as to the function of Fedallah and the phantom crew; the function of the various "gams" and of the cluster of chapters beginning with "Monstrous Pictures of Whales" (ch. 55); the function of the various images of lines and ropes and of killing, cutting, and eating. We also usually talk about why Melville thought it necessary to include the book's many cetological chapters—more than 25 out of 135. Even when the class fails to see that these chapters give Ahab's antagonist its epic proportions, most students recognize it is here that the book gains much of its meditative cast and that Ishmael's (and Melville's) imagination finds its most characteristic expression. The whale is, after all, not simply a symbol; it is a synecdoche for the whole world. Ishmael's persistent attempt to know it and understand it, therefore, mirrors humanity's perennial attempt to know and understand the alien world it inhabits but cannot call home—a world the transcendentalists called the "Not Me," or simply nature.

From the difficulties of pursuing whales, the major subject of the third day, we move on the fourth day to look at the rewards of capturing them (something that can be accomplished in the literal sense), as seen in "The Great Heidelberg Tun" (ch. 77), "The Honor and Glory of Whaling" (ch. 82), and "The Doubloon" (ch. 99), to name only the more important examples (see also chs. 78–80, 89–92, and 94–97). And we look, too, at the hazards of trying to capture them, as seen in "The Fountain" (ch. 85), "The Castaway" (ch. 93), and "The Pequod Meets the Samuel Enderby of London" (ch. 100). Because the chapters in this section are concerned primarily with the stimulation and satisfaction (or frustration) of desire—with the securing of what Joseph Campbell calls "boon" or treasure, the object of the quest—this is the day we return to the subject of *Moby-Dick* as a romance. Whether in the romanticism course or the novel course, my students have already studied this term in connection with the writings of Hawthorne, so they are prepared to discuss Melville's book as an example of the genre. Again I use the blackboard, this time to record student descriptions of the key romance elements found in both authors' narratives (and of the fundamental differences between them). But I also lecture on this subject, relying on Richard Chase's *The American Novel and Its Tradition*, the collection of primary writings in Stanley Bank's *American Romanticism: A Shape for Fiction*, and Frye's *The Secular Scripture*.

Given that much of the business of the romance, in Frye's scheme, concerns the struggle of the hero to discover his true identity, I look closely at "A Squeeze of the Hand," which constitutes the chief turning point in Ishmael's development. Here he disengages himself from Ahab's vengeful quest—and from the magnetic Ahab himself, the man who, temporarily canceling out Queequeg's influence, had become Ishmael's imprisoning "double"—in favor of fellow feeling and the "attainable" felicities of home and hearth, of the land (349; ch. 94). The next chapter but one, "The Try-Works," amply demonstrates that Ishmael has emerged from his own nightmarish "trying out" of the soul a firm believer in "the glorious, golden, glad sun" that is the "only true lamp," while at the same time he embraces the dark wisdom of "unchristian Solomon's" view that "All is vanity" (354–55; ch. 96). In Ishmael's about-face, strongly qualified as it is, we find an important example of the dialectic character of Melville's imagination, of his fascination with the contraries in life that are the subject of romance, as Frye defines it. *Moby-Dick* is a deeply divided book; it rages with conflicts, as its author raged—and marveled—at the difficulty of their resolution. Land/sea, sickness/health, blindness/vision, day/night, man/nature, matter/spirit, isolation/friendship, comedy/tragedy, sanity/madness, time/eternity, male/female, God/Satan, life/death, black/white—these are but some of the prominent polarities in Melville's book. As he later exclaimed in his poem "Art," "What unlike things must meet and mate: / A flame to melt—a wind to freeze; / Sad patience—joyous energies . . ." (Warren 335).

Having found himself and squeezed hands "all round" with his fellow shipmates, Ishmael in chapter 94 is starkly counterbalanced by Pip in the companion chapter, "The Castaway," where the story is told of how the little cabin boy so loses himself at sea as to become "mad." Consistent with the fundamental activity of all romances, in Frye's scheme, Pip is always thereafter shown as searching for his lost self. He is important, therefore, for what he reveals about the potential dangers of landlessness, but he is also important for what he reveals about the recurring theme of perception. For his soul having been "carried down alive to wondrous depths" (347; ch. 93), where he is witness to the mute, apparently meaningless processes of the natural realm, Pip is the book's image of the insane man Ishmael would have become if he had ever grown certain of the intrinsic whiteness of the world. When Pip later appears in chapter 99 he provides no reading of the doubloon; what he offers instead, when he conjugates the verb "to look," is a riddling interpretation of the readings provided by several other characters. Speaking in the tradition of Shakespeare's wise fool, Pip seems to express "man's insanity," but he utters "heaven's sense" instead (347). In "The Doubloon," he discloses the sheer vanity of all attempts to know—a variation of the wisdom of ancient Solomon. All views, he insinuates, whether of coins or whales or the world at large, display the subjectivity of the viewer. All those who come on stage in this chapter (significantly, Ishmael is not among them) are as blind as "bats"; only Pip is a "crow," as he says, because only he recognizes the relativity of all perceptions, of all ideas; only he sees through to the inherent blankness of the universe (362). Such an understanding makes him, then, an even more modern figure than Ishmael is. For Pip sees what Wallace Stevens would later show in "Thirteen Ways of Looking at a Blackbird," or what Faulkner later demonstrated in his novel of many narrators, *As I Lay Dying*, or what, more recently, Thomas Kuhn has argued in *The Structure of Scientific Revolutions*, namely, that reality is essentially a hypothetical construct, the meaning of which varies with the viewer's angle of vision.

The main subjects in the final section, chapter 102 and following, are death and survival, mutability and persistence, destruction and restoration. There is, that is to say, a lot of action in the late chapters; and action—action of a certain kind, action that includes "Peripeties and Discoveries," as Aristotle argued—is the "end and purpose," the "life and soul" of tragedy

(632–33). Because a lot happens in these pages and all at last comes to an end, I structure the day's discussion around a series of questions concerning the book's plot and ending, but I formulate them so as to encourage students to consider the conscious design of Melville's narrative: Why did Melville choose to have Ahab fail in his quest to destroy the great white whale? Does Ahab qualify as a tragic hero? Does the book as a whole qualify as a tragedy? Are there ways in which *Moby-Dick* should be thought to be a peculiarly American tragedy? At some point in the discussion I usually offer an outline of Aristotle's theory of tragedy and then a summary of Frye's conception of the genre as presented in *Anatomy of Criticism*. In line with the latter theory, I emphasize the idea that Ahab could be regarded as one who, in attempting to conquer the whale, violates natural law (or possibly super-natural law), and is at last destroyed because that law is more adamant than any human can ever be. But I also like to suggest that Ahab might be seen instead as straying too far *into* the natural order, whose law Melville defined as the "universal cannibalism of the sea" (235; ch. 58). Ahab is thus destroyed not because he violates nature's law but because he permits himself to be ruled by it, as he is ruled by his own raging passion.

The last question we consider is, why did Melville choose to have Ishmael survive—that is, why Ishmael and not some other, possibly worthier char-acter, such as Queequeg or Pip? I ask the question in this way to defeat a natural tendency of even accomplished readers to explain Ishmael's survival on the ground that, having decided in "A Squeeze of the Hand" to pull back from Ahab's fiery hunt, he is worthier of life than the others on the *Pequod*. Instead, I encourage my students to consider the possibility that Melville, in the end, did not subscribe to the popular belief that life is fair or just, that good things happen only to people who are good and evil things only to people who deserve them. When looking at the epilogue for evidence of Ishmael's own explanation of his survival, what one finds is the language of "Fate" and "chance"—"chance," Ishmael had observed in "The Mat-Maker," "has the last featuring blow at events" (185)—and a tone of humility and wonder. In the end, Ishmael afloat on the coffin is an image of the inscrutable life force, an image of us all. Like him, we are unaccountably, miraculously living; like him, we have somehow survived the previous moment; like him, we are somehow protected from surrounding dangers, somehow sustained by our own "coffin life-buoy"—the round globe of earth that supports us in the surrounding "sea" and will someday hold our remains. Mysteriously, miraculously, Ishmael has achieved the effect that Joseph Campbell says the successful hero always manages to achieve, namely, "the unlocking and release again of the flow of life into the body of the world" (40). What I find remarkable about a reading of the end of *Moby-Dick* that is informed by Campbell's *The Hero with a Thousand Faces* is this: it explains in concrete yet powerfully suggestive terms what most readers of the book feel, namely, that Ishmael is a universal hero, that *Moby-Dick* is a story of profound human longings and mysterious natural and supernatural forces, and that Melville had broken through to a deep understanding of the images that foretell humanity's fate. No passage of criticism about *Moby-Dick* known to me reveals quite so much, I think, about the meaning of the quest, of the whale, and of Melville's book as a whole as the following paragraph from Campbell's chapter "The World Navel." Most of the essentials of the closing pages are there—the whale, the vortex, the sea, the hawk, the ship with its cross or mast, its tree of life, on which is nailed the doubloon that is (as Pip recognized) an apt image of the "ship's navel," minted as it was in Ecuador, "a country planted in the middle of the world" (363, 359; ch. 99). I end by reading the passage aloud to the class:

> The torrent pours from an invisible source, the point of entry being the center of the symbolic circle of the universe, the Immovable Spot of the Buddha legend, around which the world may be said to revolve. Beneath this spot is the earth-supporting head of the cosmic serpent, the dragon, symbolical of the waters of the abyss, which are the divine life-creative energy and substance of the demiurge, the world-generative aspect of immortal being. The tree of life, i.e., the universe itself, grows from this point. It is rooted in the supporting darkness; the golden sun bird perches on its peak; a spring, the inexhaustible well, bubbles at its foot. . . . [Or] the figure may be that of the cosmic man or woman (for example the Buddha himself, or the dancing Hindu goddess Kali) seated or standing on this spot, or even fixed to the tree (Attis, Jesus, Wotan); for the hero as the incarnation of God is himself the navel of the world, the umbilical point through which the energies of eternity break into time. Thus the World Navel is the symbol of the continuous creation; the mystery of the maintenance of the world through that continuous miracle of vivification which wells within all things. (40–41)

Notes on Teaching *Moby-Dick*

Jane Mushabac

What kind of book is *Moby-Dick*? The main difficulty is expecting it to be a novel in the sense of an English novel. Read, for example, the opening page of *Silas Marner*. The sentences are a little long and complex, the surroundings are most likely unfamiliar, but something else is very familiar: the beginning of a story. The hush of complexity, even the evocation of a distant time and place, helps create a quiet space to hear a story, and the story begins in earnest, as it should, with setting and character. Our expectations are clear.

But on the opening page of *Moby-Dick*, what do we have? Not a story, but an etymology. Our reaction may well be astonishment, for it's not just an etymology but an absurd etymology provided by an absurd late schoolteacher who not only dusted his lexicons and grammar books but loved to dust them. Instead of earnest expositions, there's a wry authorial unruliness that throws the reader into confusion.

Moby-Dick is a different kind of novel from *Silas Marner*. Both books tell important, moving stories. But in *Moby-Dick* the reader shouldn't expect a calm and straightforward narration of that story. Rather, if we learn anything from the first page, it is to expect to be dazzled, admonished, hoaxed, played with, thrown this way and that—sometimes from sentence to sentence—and ultimately made wiser. Melville's seeming inanity is never just whimsy, a frothy absurdity. Nor is it "learned wit," a froth stained with tincture of iodine. The etymology, after all, is not inane but true (for the most part), appropriate (providing background on a main character of the book), and wonderful, hinting at the grand history of humankind, from the Hebrews to the Erromangoans—a quick rundown of civilizations.

Moby-Dick is not a traditional English novel, told with decorum by an inconspicuous narrator. It is a discourse, but instead of a formal, orderly, extended expression of thought on a subject, it is a formal, disorderly, extended one. It deliberately jumbles together many different kinds of prose; it is an extravagant monologue by a talker at the center of his tale. Ishmael makes fun of discourse, of readers' expectations that prose will teach them what to do, how the world is put together, how to live, how to proceed. Ishmael deliberately turns those expectations on their heads, yet after all, he does tell us coherently and forcefully what to do, how to live, how to proceed.

The goal in the classroom is to create a receptive atmosphere, getting students to notice their own reactions and not be afraid of them and yet not expect to sort out each one immediately. Question cards work well: each week students write out a few trivial and one or two important questions on an index card and hand them in. Short papers, class discussion, and several background lectures from the teacher are also important.

Here are some questions and responses: What are the exasperations of this book? The confusion, the length, the endless allusions, a sense that a grim ending lies ahead. What are the pleasures? Being told that America matters, that it is not only as prestigious and cultured as Europe but also democratic, drawing its wonders from all the races on earth. Being told the mind is wonderful; we can keep up with Melville's fast-talking holding forth because as often as not he's just teasing us, and all "learnedness" is in good part hoax. Finding Queequeg and Ishmael wonderful in their friendship, whales magnificent, the universe beautiful and endlessly mystifying. Finally, it is a keen satisfaction sensing that a very grim ending lies ahead, learning that you cannot do what Ahab tries to do.

What are the students', the teacher's, and Melville's attitudes to reading, studying, improvement, progress? These are wonderful, what a fine opportunity, we learn more and more, we become better and better. Malarkey, the whale has no face, the more you scientifically try to capture the whale, the more likely that he will get you, learning is farce, primitive Queequeg is most civilized, happiness isn't—to quote the interrogatory punch line of a long joke about an earnest man who travels the world seeking a wise man who can tell him what happiness is—a well.

What does a person feel when picking up a book or walking into a room full of books? Excitement, optimism, well-being, awe? Or trepidation, I want to go back to sleep, the last thing I want to know is how to live or what to think. Most of us have both sets of feelings. Meville starts from the latter. Indeed, setting the tone for the whole book, his first page teases his reader with an image of books left so long on their shelves that the fool who loves to dust them is not only "mildly" reminded of his mortality, but dies (1; "Etymology"). From the first, he suggests that books (schoolteachers as well, of course) are absurd, even moronic, so we are not surprised later at one of the finest images in *Moby-Dick*—Queequeg with a large book in his lap, counting its pages by fifties, letting go "a long-drawn gurgling whistle of astonishment" (51; ch. 10). But ultimately, what Melville makes fun of he marvels at: the give and take of reader and writer, the generosity and sociability, the willingness to be made a fool of—something that Ishmael has in supreme measure but that Ahab lacks disastrously.

By the way, if you're talking about the ways *Moby-Dick* is deliberately bewildering, you don't need extraneous confusions. With the Norton edition, even at the risk of saying the obvious, it's good to point out that the two historical maps at the beginning are not part of *Moby-Dick*. I wish the editors of this fine edition hadn't placed them there; they disrupt the integrity of Melville's disorderliness. And if you are using the appealing Signet edition and correcting "Peleg" on page 87—it should of course read "Bildad," and this error occurs vexingly just as readers feel they have gotten their bearings—look at a textual history of *Moby-Dick* and chat with students about errors in a five-hundred-page book written without typewriter, word processor, university salary, NEH grant, or the possibility of movie rights, just a fierce energy and an indispensable family support system.

The question may come up, where did Melville get the idea to write this kind of book—an antidiscourse discourse, an exuberant grim anatomy-monologue—instead of a traditional English novel? He had models: Rabelais, Burton, Sterne, Lamb, and others (see Mushabac; Frye, *Anatomy*; Perry Miller; and Chase, *Herman Melville*). You might want to read some of Rabelais aloud—perhaps the few pages in which Panurge wins Pantagruel's heart by introducing himself in thirteen languages (the same number of languages, by the way, in Melville's etymological overture)—to get an idea of the peremptory, playful mockery of and pleasure in learning; the religious-irreligious spirit; the cherishing of a male friendship; the grim practical jokes; the throwing together of many different kinds of prose—playing off the Bible, sermons, hymns, and prayers, building on national folk legends, and wonderfully jumbling the erudite and the slang, the happy and the grim. You might read some essays of Lamb's, weigh Burton's *Anatomy of Melancholy*, read one of its outlandish paragraphs, look at the opening of *Tristram Shandy*. But this isn't to say any odd or risqué miscellany is relevant. Specifically, I wouldn't drag in Carlyle's *Sartor Resartus* or Joyce's *Ulysses*—both of these books are characterized by a pride in intellect that undermines both the playfulness and the grimness. But besides that, Melville, like Rabelais, Burton, and Lamb before him, has a visionary coherence, a confrontation with mortality, that the word "miscellany" does not begin to convey.

But if this kind of prose plays off and builds on the Bible on one hand—and pedestrian, lowbrow, and folk materials on the other—and if the students, unlike readers in Melville's day, know little about either, they would do well to read Genesis 16–25, Jonah, 1 Kings 16–22, Job, and Luke 16.19–31. Or at least tell them the story of Sarah, Hagar, Ishmael, and Isaac (the Norton edition footnote needs a correction, by the way—it talks only about negative aspects of the Ishmael story and leaves out that he shall bring forth a great nation); tell the story of Ahab; and have them read Jonah (besides, they'll never read a finer short story), the opening and closing of Job, and the Luke excerpt. Students are relieved to have the biblical stories as a kind of cushion against the modern world; it's such a relief to know there was another world, another culture, before the American era. It's also easier to read *Moby-Dick* if some of the characters' names sound familiar.

At the other end of the spectrum from the superliterary is the subliterary. You might look at the Owen Chase excerpt in the Norton and at Vincent's chapter on Melville's fish documents and discuss the way Melville used factual sources to flesh out his memories, as well as to make fun of pompous inaccuracies about the wonders of the universe. Also, students are fascinated by how literature is put together. They like to be in on this. See the Battenfeld essay in the Norton edition, and talk about borrowing, but be careful to distinguish between borrowing and plagiarism. Rewriting a biblical tale was certainly standard; Father Mapple isn't plagiarizing the Bible in his sermon, nor is Melville in that chapter. It's not just that he gives credit but simply that other periods did not share the fetishistic concern with originality that characterizes our own times. Rather, they held the idea that a few sacred truths need to be told over and over again.

What about Hawthorne? Too much has been made of the Hawthorne-Melville relation; coming to Melville depending heavily on the Hawthorne connection is problematic. In my view, Hawthorne represented two things to Melville: first, an American ambitious of writing a real literary masterpiece, and second, a fear that it was sacrilegious, even immoral, to entertain this kind of ambition—to devote one's life to what is, after all, worldly and egotistical (despite its patriotic coloring). In short, the two men had ambition and a keen sense of ambition as sin. Aside from these similarities, Hawthorne and Melville were very different kinds of writers, writing in different traditions.

Talk about Melville's life, prominent family, grandfathers, adventures, mother's versus father's religion (see the fine biographical sections in Herbert, although he is weak on interpretation), conflicts about ambition. See Updike's piece in *Hugging the Shore* to dispel some melodramatic notions about Melville's eventual silence. In addition, debunk the homosexual myth, if it comes up, as fetishistic. Queequeg and Ishmael having a cozy bedtime chat isn't homosexual or any other kind of sexual. When, in one of his films, Charlie Chaplin goes to sleep with a drunk (male) millionaire, nobody thinks "aha! a homosexual" (and his elegantly feminine ballet in the men's locker room in another film doesn't make him transsexual either). Comedy has weddings; humor has absurd asexual hugs. Melville was writing about asexual hugs, ambition, anger, and humor.

One final subject needs a brief background lecture: the high jinks of *Moby-Dick*. The first half of the 1800s in America was a time of great excitement about progress, populism, science, democracy, America, and America's new wildly successful industry, whaling. *Moby-Dick* gives us America at a particular moment, before grim reality revealed itself with the Civil War, although Melville clearly saw the war coming. Compare that moment's trends to current waves, current excitements; what things or ideas are we wildly optimistic about, and how are they absurd or worse, or are we more in a depressive stage than a manic one? Melville saw and felt both sides; that's what humor is, the fantastic triumph and the grim reality in absurd, endless, irrepressible alternation.

Who's afraid of *Moby-Dick*? Who isn't (or as Melville would put it, ain't) afraid of *Moby-Dick*? What an intimidating book! It's not just a Miltonic or Shakespearean literary masterpiece, it's not just a mythic story of one man's exasperation. As readers we have the sense that Melville is up to tricks, contradicting himself and us, teasing us, playing with us. It's hard to get our bearings.

Perhaps it is easier for an outsider, say a Jewish woman (like this writer), to read *Moby-Dick*, because there is none of that fear, "I am American, white, Christian, male; I'm supposed to understand it." Rather, there's a skepticism, first of all (perhaps there is always a skepticism about something written by one of the opposite sex). Then there is an identification with Ishmael as outsider and with the whole book as written by an American as outsider. For when this book was written, America was the outsider—that is, it was considered second-rate compared to Europe (and still is; for instance, in certain circles, American history doesn't have the academic prestige of European history, and American literature is also still looked down on as unprestigious, upstart, possibly shoddy).

But one of the ultimate pleasures of *Moby-Dick* is that in it Melville puts America, outsider, on top. This is one of the pleasures of comedy, as Edith Kern has taught us (see *The Absolute Comic*). Sub-sub is on top! And so Ishmael and Lazarus are the wry survivors. The dumb brute Moby Dick is not so dumb after all. America is on top with its mighty whalers. Others have denigrated whaling, but Melville puts whalers in the range with Greek mythological heroes and English national saints, just as he makes Queequeg a George Washington. And ultimately the creatural is on top of the mental. "Would that I could clear out Hampton Court and the Tuileries for ye," sub-sub, says Ishmael in "Extracts" (2), and he does clear them out, for whales and fools. Creatural pleasures and creatural realisms are thrown in the face of pompous, authoritarian, scientific knowledge, just as poor Ishmael survives the mighty captain Ahab. The creatural wins!

This is the fascination of the book for women, because, first of all, the primal (primitive) is on top. The book makes fun of male, intellectual, authoritarian pretensions and aggressions; it makes fun of men, like Lina Wertmüller's wry summary of great male thinkers through history, of men's intellectual pretensions and egotistical sublimities (191).

But then, too, women aren't just primal. Women are ambitious too. You don't have to be male to be rationalistic, pretentious, authoritarian, intellectual. What woman isn't (ain't) ambitious these days? And then again, what is Ahab but a man trying to prove he's not an outsider in the universe but an insider with control? So the book speaks to everyone's ambition, aggression, and determination to make it. It speaks clearly: "Look not too long in the face of the fire" (354; ch. 96). Outsiders are often dying to be insiders—in

Moby-Dick they are literally dying, as Queequeg dies because of his curiosity about Christendom. Everyone is both an outsider and an insider. Melville laughs at and reveals the folly of human aggressive reflexes and at the same time indulges those very reflexes in writing *Moby-Dick*. He laughs at human ambition and at the same time knows his was the worst, as bad as can be; he was even frightened by the extent of his ambition, his determination to write a book that would fail in his own time but succeed wildly in posterity.

The mistake would be to approach *Moby-Dick* thinking you are an insider and should understand. Instead, you should teach or read it from whatever feeling you have of being an outsider—because you are All But Dissertation, let's say; or if a professor, untenured; or if a tenured or distinguished professor, not a lawyer making $150,000 a year; or if a lawyer making $150,000 a year, not able to fix your car or braid you daughter's hair. Who isn't an outsider, who isn't a slave?

In fact the coherence of *Moby-Dick* is its suggestion that the reader had better be able to accept a lot of incoherence, had better have a sharp sense of woe and a ready sense of humor.

Reading *Moby-Dick*: *The Whale* as Lexicon

Donald Wolff

> Having already described him in most of his present
> habitatory and anatomical peculiarities, it now remains
> to magnify him in an archaeological, fossiliferous, and
> antediluvian point of view. Applied to any other crea-
> ture than the Leviathan—to an ant or flea—such
> portly terms might justly be deemed unwarrantly
> grandiloquent. But when Leviathan is the text, the
> case is altered. Fain am I to stagger to this emprise
> under the weightiest words of the dictionary. And
> here be it said, that whenever it has been convenient
> to consult one in the course of these dissertations, I
> have invariably used a huge quarto edition of Johnson,
> expressly purchased for that purpose; because that fa-
> mous lexicographer's uncommon personal bulk more
> fitted him to compile a lexicon to be used by a whale
> author like me.
> —from "The Fossil Whale" (378–79; ch. 104)

The first page of *Moby-Dick* plunges the reader into the fluid, unsettled world of words. In "Etymology," the "late consumptive usher" provides three derivations for the word "whale," but the last two offer different origins. The grammarian also provides a list of words meaning whale in various languages, but the last two are Melville's inventions, not idiomatic Polynesian as the list pretends (Feidelson; *Moby-Dick* 6, n3). While a lexicographer's concern for etymology, semantics, denotation and connotation is central to *Moby-Dick*, the first page does not promise clear sailing.

In *Moby-Dick* words prove slippery, and the meaning often gets away. As evidence from the book mounts, students begin to see the limitations of strict adherence to denotation and quickly come to appreciate connotation, opening themselves to the ambiguities of language. But this view of language, so readily embraced by students, is marked by an openness to interpretation that too easily becomes synonymous with "anything goes" and a defense of explication based on "that's *my* opinion." The ensuing search for symbols can become so idiosyncratic that it undermines the chances for communicating about the book, for forming a community of readers and arriving at a common response. As teachers, we want our students to be open to the allusiveness of language and literature, while at the same time attending to the words themselves. We want students to avoid throwing out the book with the bathwater of literal-minded reading.

One means of sending them back to the text is to use a concept adapted from transformational grammar that attempts to describe the way denotations, connotations, and even syntactic and grammatical uses of words are delimited. I am referring to a concept defined in the last chapter of Noam Chomsky's *Aspects of the Theory of Syntax*; I make special use of two sections—"The Boundaries of Syntax and Semantics" and "The Structure of the Lexicon" (148–93). In an oversimplified form, the ideas involved are as follows: One aspect of our language is its lexicon—all the words available for use in communication. Each word has certain lexical features that delimit both meaning and syntactic or grammatical use. In a closely defined linguistic context, certain semantic and syntactic features for each word in a given statement are relevant while others are not. One can list these features and in doing so can see how context governs meaning.

To show the usefulness of this concept in reading *Moby Dick*, I begin by analyzing a comment Melville made about the book. After completing it, he wrote to Hawthorne: "I have written a wicked book, and feel spotless as the lamb" (Hayford and Parker 566). To show how a word's lexical features, along with its context, help determine meaning, I put the following on the blackboard:

a lamb   The Lamb   the lamb.

Then I solicit descriptions of the first term, which usually fall into two categories: lambs in the field (a mammal, a young sheep, black noses, white wool, grazing, lamb smells, Easter dinner, etc.) and lamblike qualities (innocence, purity, whiteness, meekness, sweetness, softness, cuddliness, etc.). That is, students provide denotative and connotative descriptions of the word's meanings.

Now we are ready to look at the second term, "The Lamb," which evokes the pastoral connotations along with a new group of lexical features, a different system of meaning. I refer of course to the Bible, where Christ is the Lamb of God. Students can now begin to see how two or more systems of meaning inform one another and determine the meaning of a given word in a specific context. They can also begin to understand Melville's use of the term in his letter. There, it is important to note, Melville did not say he felt spotless as "The Lamb." While the word "the" evokes the religious usage and establishes the allusion, the lowercase *el* used for "lamb" recalls the more secular first term. Melville thus creates his own lexicon in which he does not confuse himself with Christ, but sees in his experience a certain aspect of Christ's life.

While the preceding use of "lexicon" as a metaphor for tradition or any coherent system of meaning is not sanctioned by transformational theory, it nevertheless proves helpful in discussing metaphor, allusion, and discourse in *Moby-Dick*. This approach fascinates students, for it quantifies a reading technique they usually find mysterious and their instructors find second nature. It involves them in close reading and steers them away, as in the case of Melville's letter, from a "symbolic" reading that attempts to finish off a text neatly and cleanly; that is, they are less likely to say Melville is a symbol for Christ, or Ishmael for wandering, and be done with it. This view of allusions in *Moby-Dick* also gives students a sense of why Melville named his figures the way he did and introduces them to Melville's particular version of modernism, in which the old names still had relevance but the circumstances were new. Perhaps they will also sense Melville's unending struggle for a language adequate to experience, his search for meaning and expression as he confronted the secular and religious thought of his time.

This approach can also help students appreciate other kinds of allusions. In chapter 14, Ishmael meditates on the wonder occasioned by the sheer bulk of the whale and the incredible effort required to hunt it. He refers to the whale as "[t]hat Himmalehan, salt-sea Mastodon" (62). Here two sets of lexical features are brought together in a single phrase, linked by a reference to the omnipresent "salt-sea," the ocean that prompts Ishmael's inaugural ruminations in "Loomings." "Himmalehan" suggests the almost unimaginable height and mass of Mount Everest, with its hoary peak, and prepares us for the later meditation on the whiteness of the whale. "Mastodon" also suggests the immense bulk and prehistoric roots of the whale, perhaps hinting at Moby Dick's ubiquity in time as well as space. In this way, Melville emphasizes the great challenge presented not only in fighting whales, the ostensible subject of the chapter, but also in describing and imagining them. As my epigraph insists, only polysyllables, superlatives, and the largest dictionary are appropriate for the task.

The linguistic concept of the lexicon can be used not only to encourage close reading but also to look at larger aspects of the book, even proving helpful with one of the most problematic chapters—"Cetology." The purpose of this chapter is to dwell for a time on "a matter almost indispensable to a thorough appreciation of the more general leviathanic revelations and allusions of all sorts which are to follow," to provide "some systematized exhibition of the whale in his broad genera" (116). The narrator believes that the naturalists who previously attempted this feat were stymied by its immensity, needlessly complicating the task. He names them and suggests that most of them failed because they lacked the personal experience with their subject that would ensure accuracy. Only one of them, it seems, "was a real professional harpooner and whaleman" (117). For this reason, the central issue is clouded and, as with "Etymology," the very basis for procedure seems to be in question—"it still remains a moot point whether a whale be a fish" (118).

Nevertheless, with the confidence of Jonah, whom he mentions, the narrator plunges ahead and simply asserts that "a whale is *a spouting fish with a horizontal tail*" (119; Melville's italics). Ishmael attempts to employ both the language of common sense and the language of science in this chapter, in order to mediate the apparently contradictory worlds of everyday experience and academic learning. Ishmael's ironic treatment of previous research, his pseudoscientific posturing, point to common sense in matters of science, while his criticism of previous research itself has a scientific tone. The narrator wants his view to carry authority because he is a whaleman and speaks from experience and because he has access to facts that were unknown to previous researchers.

But the whale is not so easily classified, even with the help of a large fund of personal experience and a pseudoscientific outlook. The narrator finds he must employ another system of meanings, a lexicon that impinges on or governs both common sense and the desire to be scientific—it has to do with the world of printing, the world of books:

> First: According to magnitude I divide the whales into three primary
> BOOKS (subdivisible into CHAPTERS), and these shall comprehend
> them all, both small and large.
>   I. The FOLIO WHALE; II. the OCTAVO WHALE; III. the DUODECIMO
> WHALE.   (120)

The concept of the lexicon makes it easier to see the way Melville intends to unite these different systems of meanings, these different lexicons. The chapter brings three kinds of discourse together, employing features of each to present the whale "in his broad genera." First, the world of scientific discovery and classification provides the title and impetus for this chapter and the others that attempt to describe the whale in its immense natural detail. Second, the whaleman's world of practical experience and common sense provides a working definition of the whale as a *"spouting fish with a horizontal tail."* And third, the world of books, which may prove the most important of all, indicates that the "leviathanic revelations and allusions . . . which are to follow" include not only subsequent references to the whale in the novel but also the entire history of human experience with the whale as we know it from books. That is, the world of books not only informs Melville's attempt to classify the whale in "Cetology" but lies behind all the allusions, literary or other, that inform almost every sentence and word of *Moby-Dick*. The novel is a book of books, a text of texts, a lexicon of lexicons.

The concept of the lexicon is also useful in understanding other parts of this famous chapter, for it helps further explain how we name and the significance naming has. Take for example the end of the paragraph on the killer whale: "Exception might be taken to the name bestowed on this whale, on the ground of its indistinctness. For we are all killers, on land and sea; Bonapartes and Sharks included" (125). That is, the lexical features of "killers," "Bonapartes," and "Sharks" overlap. Facts, in the transcendentalist manner, never appear without their human lesson, and many passages in the book can reveal this kind of truth, where famous military figures all share in the chilling connotations attending "shark."

The approach also provides help with what the editors of the Norton edition describe as the "famous" final paragraph of chapter 32 (118n). The paragraph reads:

> Finally: It was stated at the outset, that this system would not be here, and at once, perfected. You cannot but plainly see that I have kept my word. But I now leave my cetological System standing thus unfinished, even as the great Cathedral of Cologne was left, with the crane still standing upon the top of the uncompleted tower. For small erections may be finished by their first architects; grand ones, true ones, ever leave the copestone to posterity. God keep me from ever completing anything. This whole book is but a draught—nay, but the draught of a draught. Oh, Time, Strength, Cash, and Patience! (127–28)

The passage is famous partly for its reflexivity, for what it suggests about the composition of the book. It seems to describe how the book comes together for the reader, piece by piece, and humorously acknowledges the venture's tentativeness. In terms of the concept I have been presenting, the passage suggests that the lexical features that help define the whale will continue to build. Furthermore, it expresses the optimistic side of mediation, of living among things and in the midst of life—"God keep me from ever completing anything."

The other side of the question, the less optimistic side of mediation, is no doubt best expressed in chapter 42, "The Whiteness of the Whale." After the celebration of process and even of incompletion at the end of "Cetology," this famous chapter explores the terror that can accompany the indistinct and unsettled in language and experience. Here, the concept of the lexicon again helps students come to grips with one of the more figurative chapters in the book. For what else is the chapter but a step-by-step meditation on the various lexical features of the word "white"? We are ineluctably led to see that the word "white" because of "its indefiniteness . . . shadows forth the heartless voids and immensities of the universe, . . . a colorless, all-color of atheism" (169). Charting the meaning of the word as it builds paragraph by paragraph in this chapter would serve as a strong introduction to the lexicon and show how Melville's rhetoric, Ishmael's perspective on lan-

guage and experience, steers the reader in a certain direction—always toward
a realization of the emotional and linguistic tension caused by the apparent
failure of traditional religion fully to explain human experience. The meditation on "white" becomes a meditation on the loss of a central governing
principle or truth, the loss of telos.

As the novel continues, the narrator turns to other kinds of descriptions
in a continuing effort to define the whale and whaling more completely. In
chapters 55–57, he catalogs various representations of the whale, some "monstrous," some "less erroneous," some "true." He treats the reader to descriptions of the whale as it appears in paint, teeth, wood, sheet iron, stone,
mountains, and the stars. Each attempt to define, describe, or represent
has its place in the story of *Moby-Dick* and in defining the whale. Yet each
proves partial, and all the efforts prove inadequate to defining the whale in
any final sense. The ultimate meaning and nature of the whale remain indeterminate, unapproachable, suspended among the manifold views of the
leviathan presented in the book.

While all points of view are necessary in defining the whale, none proves
adequate in itself or in conjunction with the others. Finally, readers are
forced to see that even the best dictionary, the largest lexicon, will not
suffice. The effort to describe or define the whale continuously opens up
new possibilities, new approaches to the subject, and invites the use of new
"vocabularies" or "languages," to use James Guetti's terms.[1] Like the narrator's attempt at cetology, or like the Cathedral of Cologne he refers to,
the task is never completed, the copestone never set in place. As Charles
Feidelson puts it, "Ishmael's 'pursuit' of the whale is the evolution of an
image" (*Symbolism* 31). Or, in the terms I have been employing, Ishmael's
pursuit of the whale is the evolution of a lexicon. One word is added to
another, one definition or description to another, one way of looking at the
whale to another, and another, and so on.

A diagram will help students see this plurality:

Each arrow represents a different way of looking at or defining the whale.
While all are relevant, none can claim absolute authority. This lesson lies
behind "Extracts," as well, where biblical, literary, nautical, and scientific
references to the whale suggest the historical growth of the image and in-
augurate this particular whale story. It is also the lesson of chapter 99, "The
Doubloon," where each member of the crew offers his interpretation of the
meaning of the gold piece, so that the doubloon comes to represent all the

different ways of looking at it, as Feidelson points out (*Symbolism* 32). The whale remains "just" a whale, "simply" is, as a lamb is always just a lamb, or a doubloon just a doubloon. But the way we look at a whale or a lamb or a doubloon determines meaning. The whale is just a whale until interpreted or defined more fully by an act of imagination.

In *Moby-Dick*, of course, Ahab's view of the whale predominates, and it determines the course of action. But his perspective is one among many and does not carry the authority of absolute truth, since the book suggests that truth is multiform, indeterminate, and ambiguous. Ahab's perspective gains authority through the force of his personality and indomitable will, through his rhetorical command of his crew, through the power invested in his prestige as captain, through what Ishmael calls his "monomania" (160; ch. 41). While Ahab's ability to impose his will on others determines the action of the story, it does not thereby negate other perspectives. The disparate views of the whale presented by Starbuck, Stubb, Flask, and the rest of the crew, as well as those presented in Ishmael's meditations and research and in the book's endless allusions, all perform an important function. They show Ahab's view for what it is; they underscore his monomania and provide alternatives. In this way, the cetology chapters become as important as the more dramatic and adventurous chapters. The full story simply cannot be told without them.

Focusing on definition, on denotation and connotation, makes many parts of the book more accessible to inexperienced readers, sends them back to the text, immerses them in the deliquescent world of semantics, and highlights Melville's thematic concern with the radical ambiguity of language, meaning, and authority. Through continued reference to the idea of the lexicon, students begin to understand Melville's whaling story as a dictionary of human endeavor. While such an emphasis on language and perspective forces rereading, it provides a method for relating disparate sections of the book. It allows students to concentrate on concrete details rather than on the mysterious and perhaps elusive whole. Students will discover that they can say a lot about the text and still not be finished with it.

NOTE

[1]Guetti provides a fine discussion of the suspension of meaning in *Moby-Dick*. His chapters on Melville, together with Feidelson's treatment of *Moby-Dick*, determined the focus of this study.

The Spatial Imperative in *Moby-Dick*

Andrew B. Crichton

For many students, *Moby-Dick* is the first exposure to the encyclopedic mind that blends thoroughness with playful experimentation. The shifting angles of vision in Melville's masterwork reenact the process of discovery and delineate the openness of a ranging investigation of experience, activities that allow students to become independent explorers themselves. Melville's narration of an epic journey, while rooted in the Nantucket whaling industry, is a journey outside time. Partly from the significant literature on the "spatial" dimension of modern literature and partly from Isabel MacCaffrey's provocative treatment of another epic narrative, I have developed enough confidence about how to deal with the text that I have my students keep a journal in which they file away perceived connections and thereby become increasingly playful with the material, as Melville encourages. There is, then, a spatial dimension to *Moby-Dick* through which both teacher and student may approach the text.

But why space? To someone like me who views "The Pacific" as Melville's Gettysburg Address about America's future, the movement beyond the molehills of California is primarily spatial. If Steelkilt wants the excitement that was formerly available to him out west, he must go out into the Pacific. The Erie Canal has made possible the development of cities like Milwaukee; the railroad has extended the settlement to the Far West. But we should not get so involved in geography that we miss the significance of the memorialization of Benjamin Franklin's grandmother as the grande dame of whaling. Students soon realize that Melville's Leyden jars provide an interesting history of technology in America and that when we look at the *Pequod* as a factory ship, we are standing before the great Bessemer furnaces that played a crucial role in America's industrial development. Through changing perspectives, the Leyden jar can represent Ahab's "own magnetic life" (146; ch. 36) only to become St. Elmo's fire in chapter 119—what elsewhere is called "the heartless immensity" of the whole charged atmosphere (347; ch. 93).

Perspectives shift so rapidly that the narrator can move from door knockers to "the starry Cetus" in a single chapter (233; ch. 57). From the sub-sub librarian's extracts, where Melville begins playing with perspectives, we know that whales are large. A whale can occupy four acres; one requires two butcher's carts to carry its liver and needs a lasso six miles long to rope this largest of all God's creations. Recall Melville's description of the abandoned Pip: "The intense concentration of self in the midst of such a heartless immensity, my God! who can tell it?" (347; ch. 93).

Once the spatial world is opened, we begin apprehending Melville's wild shifts in perspective. Dreaming in "the face of the fire" (354; ch. 96) where try-pots are large enough to light up vast stretches of the Pacific, Ishmael has transported us far from the landed constrictions of "two enormous wooden pots painted black and suspended by asses' ears" that Mrs. Hussey uses to advertise her boarding house (64; ch. 14). One must always choose between actively interpreting a "boggy, soggy, squitchy picture" (20; ch. 3) or being lulled by a presumed exactness that Melville distrusts—it is "fifteen and a quarter minutes past one o'clock P.M. of this sixteenth day of December, A.D. 1850" (310; ch. 85). The spatial equivalent of the preceding temporal fact is that the epic confrontation between Moby Dick and Ahab takes place not only on the line, the equatorial center of the earth, but at the very point where Ahab nailed the doubloon to the mast of the *Pequod*.

In a telling passage in an unlikely place, Melville opts for an empowering intuitive sense over precise factual knowledge:

> however baby man may brag of his science and skill, and however much, in a flattering future, that science and skill may augment; yet for ever and for ever, to the crack of doom, [language echoed in Faulkner's Nobel Prize acceptance speech] the sea will insult and murder him, and pulverize the stateliest, stiffest frigate he can make; nevertheless, by the continual repetition of these very impressions, man has lost that sense of the full awfulness of the sea which originally belongs to it.   (235; ch. 58)

The passage marks Ishmael's apprenticeship under Queequeg in living in nature, a way of being that corrects his faulty civilized reliance on a mechanistic notion of progress.

The intuitive epic poetry of *Moby-Dick* provides perspectives from which students can contemplate their own experiences as they record the changes in perspective that a reading of *Moby-Dick* entails. They are, moreover, actively involved in the human situation that Melville opens for them. Let's begin with a simple example. Melville postpones for 230 pages grounding the stray fact that the whaling line is 10,440 yards long; for sixty chapters the idea gestates in the reader's mind until the moment of insight when all of Melville's line lore is focused in one dramatic sentence:

> As the line passed round and round the loggerhead; so also, just before reaching that point, it blisteringly passed through and through both of Stubb's hands, from which the hand-cloths, or squares of quilted canvas sometimes worn at these times, had accidentally dropped.   (243; ch. 61)

Through such a strategy, which Melville can adopt with any inanimate object, person, or place (note that returning to the spot in Stubb's hands where we were does not substantially clarify matters), readers quickly learn that their creative insights are being continually exercised. Thus the novel provides exercises in thinking and writing that are helpful to students both in developing their ideas and in communicating those ideas in writing.

At this point, reenter Isabel MacCaffrey. She asserts that readers, if properly conditioned, can be encouraged to mine their memories for relevant connections (72). In chapter 48 of *Moby-Dick*, the fulfillment of Elijah's prophetic warning about the shadowy figures boarding the *Pequod* shows readers that we build up impressions inductively, so that when we get to Ahab or Starbuck, we can relate the contours of their characters to those of others outside the boundaries of the book. MacCaffrey argues that good readers intuitively anticipate what continually surprises the not-so-good ones (47). She affirms that fictions aid us in understanding our own psychic reality better (86). From her argument I began to generate topics concerning the mental space of *Moby-Dick*. Armed with a concept of mental space and with the imperative to think expansively, I ask my students to consider topics similar to MacCaffrey's: imagining in concrete mental images; how *Moby-Dick* teaches us the rules by which it is to be understood; how an alert reader's imagining merges with a writer's designing silence; placing history on an equal footing with speculation; how *Moby-Dick* suggests more meaning than Melville can treat exhaustively.

My students keep a systematic notebook during our reading of *Moby-Dick*. For their running log, they designate one side of an ordinary notebook page for each entry. At the outset the notebook allows students to keep track of what is happening in the novel. Meanwhile, I encourage them to branch out—for instance, to write about Queequeg's saving power in the ferryboat rescue, Anwar Sadat's observance of Ramadan, Charles Dickens's description of Father Taylor in his *American Notes* alongside Melville's depiction of Father Mapple, references to the sea in the Isaac Watts hymns that Sister Charity distributes to the crew, and so on. By the middle of the novel, let's say chapter 48, students begin to trace the patterns of their own inductive process of comprehending the novel. That process invariably involves them in what Ricardo Gullón, building on the work of Joseph Frank, calls "mythic space" (18). Gullón quotes Samuel Alexander on the narrative description of physical objects "over there in spatial relation to our own mental space" (12). This mental or perceptual space is "homogeneous and universal," in the words of another of Gullón's sources, Ernst Cassirer (16). In such a modern novel as Melville's epic we readers create the mythic space of Ishmael's voyage that both literally and psychologically takes us around the seven seas. Reading Melville's description of the squid in chapter 59 may remind a reader of the science-fiction epic, as it did Richard Grossinger. All of Melville's iteration, parallelism, and contrast, so regularly appearing in the novel, encourages extensions like these.

Melville suggests to the journal writer both interesting compositional forms and broad thematic areas that lend themselves directly to spatial treatment. In another epic, like Spenser's *Faerie Queene*, we might talk of the writer's "painterly eye." At the rational and descriptive end of the spectrum, one might use the excellent opportunities in chapters 67 and 77 to interest the student in solid geometry—peeling an orange, cutting a quoin, and so forth. This operation can be extended by seeing chapters 102 and 103 as a short course in primitive art similar to describing totems of the Kwakiutl Indians.

At the other end of the spectrum there are free-associational and intuitive projects galore. One involves approaching chapter 79, "The Prairie," with a few additional props. You need a geological survey map of a glacial region like Mirror Lake in Colorado's Gunnison National Forest, an illustrated geology text, a picture of Shakespeare, and a description of the mid-nineteenth-century craze over phrenology. Then the students start to work on this passage:

> Few are the foreheads which like Shakespeare's or Melancthon's rise so high, and descend so low, that the eyes themselves seem clear, eternal, tideless mountain lakes; and all above them in the forehead's wrinkles, you seem to track the antlered thoughts descending there to drink, as the Highland hunters track the snow prints of the deer. (292)

Assignment: "Write on Melville's phrenology of a glacial region."

In between Melville's descriptive and free-associational modes lies his reflective writing, the key quality of which is a solitary communing with nature, as in this passage:

> But even so, amid the tornadoed Atlantic of my being, do I myself still for ever centrally disport in mute calm; and while ponderous planets of unwaning woe revolve round me, deep down, deep inland there I still bathe me in eternal mildness and joy. (326; ch. 87)

In addition to these differing modes of expression, there are a number of techniques that Melville either illustrates outright or strongly suggests to a teacher and students looking at his various working strategies. Of the latter, for example, my students need to write a letter as if I were Captain Peleg or Bildad; their task is to enumerate what skills they will bring along on our journey through the book. These abilities vary widely, from navigating without instruments to explaining Melville's art-historical references. After Queequeg rescues Tashtego, my students have assimilated the Jonah story enough that they can write their own imaginative account about what it is like to be in the belly of a whale.

Attentive to Charles Olson's perception that Melville is "wide-eyed enough to understand the Pacific as part of our geography" (16), the students read "The Pacific" along with the Gettysburg Address as two mid-nineteenth-century estimates of America's future. Melville describes the Pacific frontier as "sea pastures, wide-rolling watery prairies" (399). California towns are "moles" washed by powerful waves. Asia is older than Abraham; it contains

> float[ing] milky-ways of coral isles, and low-lying, endless, unknown Archipelagoes, and impenetrable Japans. Thus this mysterious, divine Pacific zones the world's whole bulk about; makes all coasts one bay to it; seems the tide-beating heart of the earth. Lifted by those eternal swells, you needs must own the seductive god, bowing your head to Pan. (400)

This passage further reinforces the epic qualities of the text and points to the sources of the American drive toward westward expansion. In conjunction with these readings, I ask students to explain why America could not be contained at its western border (e.g., to discuss Seward's negotiations for the purchase of Alaska) and to determine the Pacific's role in recent times as exemplified by our involvement in the Vietnam War. These procedures merely suggest the variety of spatial topics that can be explored.

A more ambitious project concerns the figural view of biblical history. One year during the Christmas season I happened to be discussing the reference to Daniel in chapter 34 of *Moby-Dick*, where the *Pequod* begins its voyage on Christmas Day (131; other references to Daniel appear on pp. 356 [ch. 98], 360 [ch. 99], 415 [ch. 119]). Noah Greenberg's musical adaptation of *The Play of Daniel*, a medieval Christmas pageant from Beauvais, seemed a natural companion work. In this context, Melville's references to Daniel reveal that his point of view resembled that of medieval writers, who saw Daniel as a person of strong faith, a figure who exemplified the loyal Christian responding to Christ's birth.

Not all the shared experiences with this text need be literary or cultural. I have as much fun demonstrating the function of a Leyden jar or winching up a bale of hay into a haymow, and I derive satisfaction from my students' responses to Melville's fascination with his physical world. To illustrate Melville's imaginative geography, I describe what I believe the alert reader should see in a passage of chapter 52 and the kind of thinking that must precede a full appreciation of chapter 83. As the *Pequod* rounds the Cape of Good Hope in chapter 52, Ishmael is imagining a Suez Canal: "Were this world an endless plain, and by sailing eastward we could for ever reach new distances, and discover sights more sweet and strange than any Cyclades or Islands of King Solomon, then there were promise in the voyage" (204). We are in the Indian Ocean thinking of how to get to islands in the South Aegean between Greece and Turkey. We can dismiss this idea as just more of Ishmael's wishful thinking, but we do so at our own peril. Actually, Ishmael is not even satisfied to leave the matter at that speculation; he must return to the world of Jonah's biblical legend and myth in chapter 83. In the final payoff, biblical myth is blended with Newtonian physics and Cartesian philosophy into a metaphysics of space. The narrator's embellishing voice thinks aloud,

> But not to speak of the passage [Jonah and the whale's] through the whole length of the Mediterranean, and another passage up the Persian Gulf and the Red Sea, such a supposition would involve the complete circumnavigation of Africa in three days, not to speak of the Tigris waters, near the site of Nineveh, being too shallow for any whale to swim in. (308)

Literalists beware. Melville's syncretic genius is at work. Whether Jonah could have fit into the head of a right whale is immaterial to Melville.

Melville's transposition of the distinction between the sea and land could make another interesting biblical assignment. We know from his "Extracts" that he was familiar with Milton's account of the mariners who mistook a whale for dry land and were dragged to the bottom of the sea (*Paradise Lost* 1.200–08). Melville quotes Obed Macy's *History of Nantucket:* "there—pointing to the sea—is green pasture where our children's grandchildren will go for bread" (8). We recall the elegiac note that leviathan "swam the seas before the continents broke water; he once swam over the site of the Tuileries, and Windsor Castle, and the Kremlin" (384; ch. 105). In chapter 23, "The Lee Shore," the same land that felt scorching to Bulkington's feet could ground the *Pequod*. Just as the "damp, drizzly November in [Ishmael's] soul" caused him to ship out to sea (12; ch. 1), so his biblical namesake was the archer whose feet were so scorched in the desert that he continually wandered (Gen. 21.20). Napoleon, Nelson, and Washington in statuary form stand watch as if on mastheads over what were formerly seas (136; ch. 35). Melville seriously speculates about the harmonic interplay of sea and land, as did the Genesis writer, who saw them as two aspects of the same thing and therefore found it unnecessary to include, between the creation of sea and of land, the refrain "And God saw that it was good."

Biblical myth and modern discovery and technology can coexist only in the mental space Melville creates in the novel. To return to MacCaffrey's terms, it is through the reader's memory that unexpressed relations are made. The reader's integrating and the writer's system building allow reader and writer each to make a new discovery and claim it as his or her own. Speculation becomes more valuable than quantification. The cognitive, while an important part of Melville's perspective, is qualified by Queequeg's intuitive, aboriginal world. Melville warned us that Kokovoko was not on any map (56; ch. 12) and that each whaleman was "a separate continent of his own" (108; ch. 27). We must conclude with Herbert Eldridge that Ahab's "miscellaneous hunt" is presented in a "simple spatial pattern" (146), which can also be described as a zigzagging journey that covers the rich mental space we inhabit.

Teaching *Moby-Dick* in the Light of Turner

Robert K. Wallace

Were there world enough and time (there seldom is in a given undergraduate course, especially at a commuter university where most students work twenty hours a week), I would prefer always to teach *Moby-Dick* in a wider frame of reference than the one provided by a traditional three-hour literature course. Team teaching is one way to expand the horizon: the most commodious vessel in which I have so far pursued the whale was a six-hour seminar on nineteenth-century America in which I shared the bridge with Michael Adams, a historian. Another way to widen the frame is to embark on one's own interdisciplinary courses. Among the three-hour courses I have taught alone, two in comparative arts have shed special light on Melville's masterpiece. The paintings of J. M. W. Turner figured prominently in both. Twelve Romantic Artists and Nineteenth-Century Fiction, Painting, and Music are seminars designed for advanced undergraduates. In each course the paintings of Turner serve as doubloons to *Moby-Dick*: they illuminate the novel and in the process are illuminated by it. Although some Melville-Turner comparisons are applicable only in interart courses, others would apply to the study of *Moby-Dick* in any classroom setting. In these pages I shall emphasize the latter.

Turner was born forty-four years before Melville, in 1775. But in the 1840s, while Melville was manning whaleboats in the South Seas and launching his career as a writer, Turner was consolidating discoveries about life and art comparable to those Melville would make while writing *Moby-Dick* (the London edition was published in October 1851, two months before Turner's death). In subject matter, Turner's four oil paintings of whaling scenes—exhibited at the Royal Academy in 1845 and 1846—obviously relate to *Moby-Dick*. More significant connections, however, can be found in these two artists' rendering of motion, their perception of color, their portrayal of man's relations to the sea and nature, their recognition that perception depends on medium, and their tragic vision. Here I can suggest only a few ways in which comparisons with Turner paintings can enrich a student's experience of *Moby-Dick*.

In chapter 3 (20–21), Ishmael contemplates the unaccountable painting in the Spouter-Inn: "A boggy, soggy, squitchy picture truly, enough to drive a nervous man distracted." His highly charged, self-reflexive language does help the reader visualize the painting itself: "But what most puzzled and confounded you was a long, limber, portentous black mass of something hovering in the centre of the picture over three blue, dim perpendicular lines floating in a nameless yeast." Ishmael finally makes out "an exasperated whale" in an "enormous act," but the reader receives a much clearer sense of Ishmael's attempt to understand the painting than of what is actually portrayed. The process by which he finally does come to apprehend this pictorial delineation of "chaos bewitched," a process complicated by the "unequal cross-lights" through which the smoke-blackened canvas must be perceived, anticipates the process by which the reader must come to apprehend the novel itself.

Students can more concretely experience Ishmael's encounter with the Spouter-Inn painting if they confront the "nameless yeast" of some of Turner's oil paintings of the 1840s—paintings termed "boggy, soggy, squitchy" (and worse) by contemporary critics but today viewed by many as the culmination of Turner's artistic development. One fine example is *Snow Storm—Steam-Boat off a Harbour's Mouth Making Signals in Shallow Water, and Going by the Lead* (1842).[1] The ship in this painting, like the one pictured in the Spouter-Inn, is enveloped in a commotion of sea and sky that holds no promise of relief. One contemporary of Turner found in this scene nothing but "soapsuds and whitewash." But Ruskin calls it, in *Modern Painters*, "one of the very grandest statements of sea-motion, mist, and light, that has ever been put on canvas, even by Turner." Ruskin points out that "there is indeed no distinction left between air and sea; . . . no object, nor horizon, nor any land-mark or natural evidence of position is left" (Butlin and Joll 214–15). The very self-reflexiveness of this work, its total departure from conventional, reliable frames of reference, gives it the sort of "indefinite, half-attained, unimaginable sublimity" that froze Ishmael to the "marvellous" painting in the Spouter-Inn (20).

The second seascape that Ishmael encounters, the one in Father Mapple's pulpit in chapter 8, presents a different view of reality. Instead of "chaos bewitched," Ishmael here sees

> a large painting representing a gallant ship beating against a terrible storm off a lee coast of black rocks and snowy breakers. But high above the flying scud and dark-rolling clouds, there floated a little isle of sunlight, from which beamed forth an angel's face; and this bright face shed a distinct spot of radiance upon the ship's tossed deck.   (43)

Father Mapple's painting is conventional, representational, and religiously inspirational. It contrasts in all these qualities with its counterpart in the Spouter-Inn, as does the diction with which Ishmael describes it. Instead of the probing, convoluted, self-reflexive language he invokes for the Spouter-Inn work, Ishmael here uses conventional, even sentimental phrases such as "gallant ship," "beamed forth," and, in the imagined exhortation from the angel, "beat on, beat on, thou noble ship." Turner's famous 1803 painting *Calais Pier* contrasts in much the same way with the chaos of *Snow Storm—Steam-Boat.* This powerful seascape has no angel in the sky, but there is an "isle of sunlight" above the "flying scud and dark-rolling clouds" that brings illumination and radiance to the men in the storm-tossed boats. *Calais Pier* is not religiously inspirational in the manner of Father Mapple's seascape, but it is dramatically representational in much the same way.

The contrast between Turner's early and late styles is equally evident in his numerous paintings of the lee shore. *Fishermen upon a Lee-Shore, in Squally Weather* (1802), though perilous, has an isle of sunlight similar to those in *Calais Pier* and the painting in Father Mapple's pulpit (itself depicting a "storm off a lee coast"). But Turner's *Waves Breaking on a Lee Shore* (1835) features, rather than the conventional isle of sunlight, an "indefinite half-attained, unimaginable sublimity" as perilous and grand as that in *Snow Storm—Steam-Boat*. Such a painting can help students visualize "The Lee Shore," chapter 23 of *Moby-Dick*, allowing them to experience more concretely the perilous grandeur of Bulkington's and Ishmael's voyages into the "howling infinite" (97).

For Turner, no less than for Melville, the voyage into the infinite led to the creation of a new aesthetic, a new way of perceiving reality. Some of the philosophical depths sounded in "The Whiteness of the Whale" have visual counterparts in paintings by Turner. Canvases as early as *Death on a Pale Horse* (c. 1825–30) depict a frightening whiteness, a color whose use in portraying indistinctness became increasingly prevalent in Turner's later work. Ishmael's contention that "this visible world seems formed in love" (169) can be illustrated by any number of Turner's gorgeous Venetian scenes; for the balancing contention that "the invisible spheres were formed in fright" there could hardly be a better illustration than Turner's *Venice with the Salute* (c. 1840–45), in which the painter empties his canvas of the certainties of shape and color he had previously rendered with such fidelity and love, leaving a shadowy, all-pervasive, atheistic white.

Many dramatic moments from the chase scenes of *Moby-Dick* can be compared with paintings by Turner that blend motion, color, and medium into one vibrating blur. The purpose of evoking Turner here is not simply to match painting and page but to explore an artist whose mode of perception matches Melville's own. In this sense, two of Turner's whaling paintings, *The Whale Ship* and *Whalers*, are worthy of comparison with the chase chapters that conclude the novel. They also invite comparison with chapters 55–57, as analogues to the kind of vision (and reality) that Ishmael vainly seeks to find in paintings and drawings of those who have tried to portray the whale and the hunt. So far as we know, Turner never witnessed a whale hunt. Even so, *The Whale Ship* and *Whalers* come closer than even Garneray's engravings to capturing the "single incomputable flash of time" that Ishmael admires in the Frenchman's portrayal of the hunt (229; ch. 56). Turner's blending of sea and sky, of ship and spray, and of white and grey in *The Whale Ship* seems to embody the kind of aesthetic for which Ishmael is searching, as does the tension Turner creates between the gushing whale in the foreground, the ghostly ship in the background, and the tiny boat suspended between them. Had Melville been able to see Turner's paintings of whales before writing *Moby-Dick*, Ishmael would surely not have dismissed English artists for presenting only "the mechanical outline of things" (230).

Beyond specific similarities of the kind outlined above, the very grandeur of Melville's undertaking has strong affinities with Turner's artistic quest. Melville's literary attempt to be all-inclusive and all-allusive has a visual counterpart in such Turner paintings as *Snow Storm: Hannibal and His Army Crossing the Alps* (1812): the brutal pillage of war in the foreground is ironically contrasted with the vista of bountiful light in the background, the minuscule figure of Hannibal on his elephant, dwarfed by the storm, being the only link between those two worlds. Other Turner paintings with such grandeur, though their multiple layers of reality make them grandiose failures by classical standards, include *The Fifth Plague of Egypt* (1800), *Ulysses Deriding Polyphemus* (1829), and *The Parting of Hero and Leander* (1837). Students who at first are intimidated by Melville's grand style sometimes find it more approachable after studying such works by Turner. No less than Melville, Turner felt that a mighty work demanded a mighty theme; he, too, was willing to make the aesthetic adjustments that such a comprehensive vision required.

In *Berlioz and the Romantic Century*, Jacques Barzun writes that "the perfection of Romanticism is to bring into a tense equilibrium many radical diversities." Such is the perfection Turner and Melville sought.

> It consequently produces work that shows rough texture, discontinuities, distortions—antitheses of structure as well as substance. From the classical point of view these are flaws; but they are consented to by the Romanticist—indeed sought after—for the sake of the drama; they are not oversights on the artist's part but planned concessions to the medium and the aim it subserves—as in engineering one finds gaps, vents or holes to balance the effects of expansion by heat or stress of vibration.   (1: 373)

This insight applies to *Moby-Dick* or to *Hannibal and His Army Crossing the Alps* as much as it does to Berlioz's *Symphonie Fantastique*. Students, even without a great deal of prior training in the arts, can intuitively grasp such stylistic insights about Melville, Turner, or Berlioz (especially in courses that have also exposed them to the classical point of view); when students write comparative papers they can methodically pursue such intuitions.

One requirement of my courses comparing the arts is that students present their own interart comparisons during the final weeks. One way to prepare them for such self-generated work is to require them to keep a running journal, or log, in response to *Moby-Dick*. A journal not only forces students to crystallize their own responses as they read but also builds into the learning process an emphasis on process itself, an approach eminently suited to the self-reflexive mode employed by Ishmael. The journal often inspires students to make connections with other courses or with personal experience that they would not have made otherwise; sometimes it produces the idea for a student's presentation. Starting with Melville and Turner, Dennis Carney explored the allure of water in words, in paint, and in life. His "Watergazers" blended his own words with those of Melville, Irving, and Conrad, his own visions with those of Turner, Cole, and Monet. Departing from the "magic streams" invoked by Ishmael in the woodland headwaters of "Loomings" (2), he pursued his ungraspable phantom into rivers, through gorges, across estuaries, and, finally, into the oceans of the world.

Although Turner's paintings cannot, in themselves, purchase enough class-room world and time in which to do justice to *Moby-Dick*, they certainly can expand the frame of reference. As classroom aids, they have consistently helped students to share Melville's vision, whatever the goals of a particular course. Two years ago, having offered six different undergraduate courses in which *Moby-Dick* figured somewhere but was never treated in sufficient depth or in a wide enough context, I designed an entire three-hour course around the book. Beginning with *Typee* and ending with *The Confidence Man*, I supplemented *Moby-Dick* with other masterworks that I felt explored comparable artistic and spiritual terrain. The non-Melvillian works were the Book of Job, *King Lear*, *The Scarlet Letter*, *Wuthering Heights*, and Turner's paintings. The "cross-lights" provided by Turner brought illumination as wide and deep as any.

NOTE

[1]All paintings by Turner discussed in this essay are reproduced in the volume of plates that accompanies Butlin and Joll.

PARTICIPANTS IN SURVEY OF *MOBY-DICK* INSTRUCTORS

The generous and perceptive insights provided by these respondents to the Modern Language Association's request for information on teaching *Moby-Dick* have contributed significantly to the creation of this volume.

Francis R. Adams, Jr., James Madison University; Joyce Sparer Adler, Vermont Academy of Arts and Sciences; William L. Andrews, University of Wisconsin, Madison; Robert P. Ashley, Ripon College; Steven Gould Axelrod, University of California, Riverside; Louise S. Bailey, Marshall University; Philip D. Beidler, University of Alabama; Millicent Bell, Boston University; Robert F. Bergstrom, University of Nebraska; Dennis Berthold, Texas A&M University; Mary Blish, University of the Sacred Heart; Alec Bond, Southwest State University; Gordon V. Boudreau, LeMoyne College; Lawrence Buell, Oberlin College; Sargent Bush, University of Wisconsin, Madison; Mary Ellen Caldwell, University of North Dakota, Grand Rapids; Jack Capps, United States Military Academy; Martin Christadler, Institut für England und Amerikastudien; John Chun, Bowling Green State University; James L. Colwell, University of Texas, Permian Basin; Dominick P. Consolo, Denison University; Charles H. Cook, Jr., Westminster College; Ethel F. Cornwell, Shepherd College; Bainard Cowan, Louisiana State University; Andrew B. Crichton, Westtown School; Curtis Dahl, Wheaton College; Donald A. Daiker, Miami University, Ohio; William F. Davis, College of William and Mary; Sharon Dean, Rivier College; Richard C. DeProspo, Washington College; Martin K. Doudna, University of Hawaii, Hilo; Phyllis Doyle, St. Joseph's College; Ken Eble, University of Utah; Heyward Ehrlich, Rutgers University; Herbert G. Eldridge, University of Colorado, Denver; Everett Emerson, University of Massachusetts, Amherst; Walter Evans, Augusta College; Joseph Flibbert, Salem State College; Allen Flint, University of Maine, Farmington; Thomas W. Ford, University of Houston; Robert H. Fossum, Claremont McKenna College; Edward Hasley Foster, Stevens Institute of Technology; Richard Lee Francis, Western Washington University; Lucy M. Freibert, University of Louisville; Steven H. Gale, Missouri Southern State College; John F. Gilgun, Missouri Western State College; Edwin Gittleman, University of Massachusetts, Boston; Arnold Goldman, University of Keele; Rita K. Gollin, State University of New York College, Geneseo; Norman S. Grabo, Texas A&M University; Susette R.

Graham, Nazareth College; Robert Gregory, Carnegie-Mellon University; Donald J. Greiner, University of South Carolina; George Grella, University of Rochester; R. K. Gupta, Indian Institute of Technology; Charles B. Hands, Loyola College; Keiichi Harada, Chiba University; Earl N. Harbert, Northeastern University; Terry Heller, Coe College; Howard C. Horsford, University of Rochester; Lisa Ann Horwitz, University of Illinois, Urbana; Marcia Jacobson, Auburn University; David Ketterer, Concordia University; Kathleen E. Kier, Queens College, City University of New York; Klaus Lanzinger, University of Notre Dame; Benjamin Lawson, Albany State College; William T. Lenehan, University of Wisconsin, Madison; Perry Lentz, Kenyon College; David Leverenz, Rutgers University; Stuart Levine, University of Kansas; Alexander Liddie, Trenton State College; Edgar Lovelady, Grace College; Eleanor Lyons, Indiana University, South Bend; Meredith Machen, Northern New Mexico Community College; Veronica Makowsky, Middlebury College; Daniel Marder, University of Tulsa; Julian Markels, Ohio State University; Sanford E. Marovitz, Kent State University; Roger E. Masse, New Mexico State University; Barbara Howard Meldrum, University of Idaho; Charles Mignon, University of Nebraska; Robert Milder, Washington University; James E. Miller, Jr., University of Chicago; Maxine Moore, University of Missouri, Kansas City; John J. Murphy, Merrimack College; Kevin Murphy, Ithaca College; Jane Mushabac, Queens College, City University of New York; Charles Nicol, Indiana State University; Ellen J. O'Brien, Guilford College; Lawrence E. Oelschlegel, St. Mary's College, Winona; Louis Oldani, Rockhurst College; Roger J. Owens, Whittier College; Marco A. Portales, University of Houston, Clear Lake City; A. James Prins, Hope College; Patrick F. Quinn, Wellesley College; Mary Louise Rea, Indiana University–Purdue University, Indianapolis; Robert D. Richardson, University of Denver; David Robinson, Oregon State University; John H. Roch, Glassboro State College; Kenneth M. Roemer, University of Texas, Arlington; Bernard Rosenthal, State University of New York, Binghamton; Richard Rust, University of North Carolina, Chapel Hill; Barton L. St. Armand, Brown University; Richard Sax, Fessenden School; Jack Scherting, Utah State University; Peter Schmidt, Swarthmore College; Richard Schneider, Atlantic Christian College; Richard Schuster, New England College; William H. Shurr, University of Tennessee, Knoxville; Merrill Skaggs, Drew University; Susan Sutton Smith, State University of New York College, Oneonta; L. Eugene Startzman, Berea College; Donald B. Stauffer, State University of New York, Albany; Christopher W. Sten, George Washington University; Gary Lee Stonum, Case Western Reserve University; Carol C. Strickland, Stevens Institute of Technology; Edwin Suvanto, Dalton School; G. M. Sweeney, University of Akron; Stephen E. Tabachnick, Ben-Gurion University of the Negev, Beersheva, Israel; Stephen Tatum, University of

Utah; Henry Terrie, Dartmouth College; Richard Tuerk, East Texas State University; David L. Vanderwerken, Texas Christian University; Kathleen Verduin, Hope College; Clyde Wade, University of Missouri; Cheryl Walker, Scripps College; Jeffrey Walker, Oklahoma State University; Ronald G. Walker, University of Houston, Victoria; Robert K. Wallace, Northern Kentucky University; Thomas F. Walsh, Georgetown University; Charles N. Watson, Syracuse University; Howard Webb, Southern Illinois University, Carbondale; Bette S. Weidman, Queens College, City University of New York; Elsie L. West, Johnson State College (retired); Harry C. West, North Carolina State University; Donald Wolff, University of California, Santa Barbara; Ann Woodlief, Virginia Commonwealth University; Delbert E. Wylder, Murray State University; Robert Zaslavsky, Bryn Mawr College

WORKS CITED

Books and Articles

Abrams, M. H. *The Mirror and the Lamp: Romantic Theory and the Critical Tradition.* New York: Norton, 1953.

Adler, Joyce Sparer. *War in Melville's Imagination.* New York: New York UP, 1981.

Allen, Gay Wilson. *Melville and His World.* London: Thames, 1971.

Alter, Robert. *Rogue's Progress.* Cambridge: Harvard UP, 1965.

Anderson, Charles R. *Melville in the South Seas.* 1939. New York: Dover, 1966.

Aristotle. *Poetics.* Trans. Ingram Bywater. *Introduction to Aristotle.* Ed. Richard McKeon. New York: Modern Library, 1947.

Arvin, Newton. *Herman Melville.* 1950. New York: Compass-Viking, 1957.

Auden, W. H. *The Enchafèd Flood; or, The Romantic Iconography of the Sea.* New York: Random, 1950.

Baird, James. *Ishmael.* 1956. New York: Harper Torchbook, 1960.

Bakhtin, Mikhail. *Problems of Dostoevsky's Poetics.* Trans. R. W. Rotsel. Ann Arbor: Ardis, 1973.

Ballou, R. O., ed. *The Bible of the World.* New York: Viking, 1939.

Bank, Stanley, *American Romanticism: A Shape for Fiction.* New York: Putnam, 1969.

Barbour, James. "The Writing of *Moby-Dick.*" Diss. U of California, Los Angeles, 1970.

Barthes, Roland. "The Structuralist Activity." *European Literary Theory and Practice.* Ed. Vernon W. Gras. New York: Dell, 1973. 157–63.

Barzun, Jacques. *Berlioz and the Romantic Century.* 3rd ed. 2 vols. New York: Columbia UP, 1969.

Beaver, Harold, ed. *Moby-Dick.* By Herman Melville. Harmondsworth: Penguin, 1972.

Beebe, Maurice, Harrison Hayford, and Gordon Roper. "Criticism of Herman Melville: A Selected Checklist." *Modern Fiction Studies* 8 (1962): 312–46.

Bell, Michael Davitt. *The Development of American Romance: The Sacrifice of Relation.* Chicago: U of Chicago P, 1980.

Bell, Millicent. "Pierre Bayle and *Moby-Dick.*" *PMLA* 66 (1951): 626–48.

Bellamy, Joseph. *The Works of Joseph Bellamy, DD.* 2 vols. Boston, 1850.

Berthoff, Warner. *The Example of Melville.* Princeton: Princeton UP, 1962.

Bezanson, Walter E. "*Moby-Dick*: Work of Art." Hayford and Parker 651–71.

Black, Stephen. "On Reading Psychoanalytically." *College English* 39 (1977): 267–74.

Bloom, Harold. *Agon: Towards a Theory of Revisionism.* New York: Oxford UP, 1982.

——. *The Breaking of the Vessels.* Chicago: U of Chicago P, 1976.

Boswell, Jeanetta. *Herman Melville and the Critics: A Checklist of Criticism, 1900–1978.* Metuchen: Scarecrow, 1981.

Bowen, Merlin. *The Long Encounter: Self and Experience in the Writings of Herman Melville.* Chicago: U of Chicago P, 1960.

Branch, Watson G., ed. *Melville: The Critical Heritage.* London: Routledge, 1974.

Braswell, William. *Melville's Religious Thought.* 1943. New York: Pageant, 1959.

Brodhead, Richard H. *Hawthorne, Melville, and the Novel.* Chicago: U of Chicago P, 1976.

Brodtkorb, Paul. *Ishmael's White World: A Phenomenological Reading of Moby-Dick.* New Haven: Yale UP, 1965.

Browne, Lewis. *The World's Greatest Scriptures.* New York: Macmillan, 1961.

Bryant, John. *Melville Dissertations, 1924–1980: An Annotated Bibliography and Subject Index.* Westport: Greenwood, 1983.

Bucke, Richard M. *Notes and Fragments Left by Walt Whitman.* London, Ont., 1899.

Buell, Lawrence. "Observer-Hero Narratives." *Texas Studies in Language and Literature* 21 (1979): 93–111.

Burke, Kenneth. *The Philosophy of Literary Form.* Rev. ed. New York: Random, 1957.

Butlin, Martin, and Evelyn Joll. *The Paintings of J. M. W. Turner. Text.* New Haven: Yale UP, 1977.

Calvin, John. *Institutes of the Christian Religion.* Trans. John Allen. New York, 1819.

Cameron, Sharon. *The Corporeal Self: Allegories of the Body in Melville and Hawthorne.* Baltimore: Johns Hopkins UP, 1981.

Campbell, Joseph. *The Hero with a Thousand Faces.* 2nd ed. 1949. Princeton: Princeton UP, 1968.

——. "Transformations of the Hero." *The Making of Myth.* Ed. Richard M. Ohmann. New York: Putnam, 1962. 99–134.

Canons of Dordt. Reformed Standards of Unity. Ed. Leroy Nixon. Grand Rapids: Soc. for Reformed Publications, 1952. 97–119.

Carlyle, Thomas. "The Hero as Divinity." 1841. *On Heroes, Hero-Worship, and the Heroic in History.* London: Dent, 1965. 239–77.

Chase, Richard. *The American Novel and Its Tradition.* 1957. Baltimore: Johns Hopkins UP, 1980.

——. *Herman Melville: A Critical Study.* New York: Macmillan, 1949.

——, ed. *Melville: A Collection of Critical Essays.* Englewood Cliffs: Prentice, 1962.

Chomsky, Noam. *Aspects of the Theory of Syntax.* Cambridge: MIT P, 1965.

Cook, Charles H., Jr. "Ahab's 'Intolerable Allegory.'" *Boston University Studies in English* 1 (1955): 45–52.

Cowan, Bainard. *Exiled Waters: Moby-Dick and the Crisis of Allegory.* Baton Rouge: Louisiana State UP, 1982.

Crane, R. S. *The Languages of Criticism and the Structure of Poetry.* Toronto: U of Toronto P, 1953.

Davis, Merrell R., and William H. Gilman, eds. *The Letters of Herman Melville.* New Haven: Yale UP, 1960.

Derrida, Jacques. *Of Grammatology.* Trans. Gayatri C. Spivak. Baltimore: Johns Hopkins UP, 1976.

DeVries, Peter. *The Blood of the Lamb.* Boston: Little, 1961.

Douglas, Ann. *The Feminization of American Culture.* New York: Knopf, 1977.

Dryden, Edgar A. *Melville's Thematics of Form: The Great Art of Telling the Truth.* Baltimore: Johns Hopkins UP, 1968.

Duban, James. *Melville's Major Fiction: Politics, Theology, and Imagination.* DeKalb: Northern Illinois UP, 1983.

Edinger, Edward F. *Melville's* Moby-Dick: *A Jungian Commentary.* New York: New Directions, 1978.

Eigner, Edwin. *The Metaphysical Novel in England and America: Dickens, Bulwer, Hawthorne, Melville.* Berkeley: U of California P, 1978.

Eldridge, Herbert G. " 'Careful Disorder': The Structure of *Moby-Dick.*" *American Literature* 39 (1967): 145–62.

Emerson, Ralph Waldo. "The Poet." *Selections from Ralph Waldo Emerson.* Ed. Stephen E. Whicher. Boston: Houghton, 1960.

———. "Self-Reliance." *The Collected Works of Ralph Waldo Emerson.* Ed. Joseph Slater, Alfred R. Ferguson, and Jean Ferguson Carr. Vol. 2. Cambridge: Belknap–Harvard UP, 1971. 27–54.

Feidelson, Charles, Jr., ed. *Moby-Dick.* By Herman Melville. Indianapolis: Bobbs, 1964.

———. *Symbolism and American Literature.* Chicago: U of Chicago P, 1953.

Fiedler, Leslie. *Love and Death in the American Novel.* 1960. Cleveland: Meridian, 1962.

Finkelstein, Dorothee M. *Melville's Orienda.* New Haven: Yale UP, 1961.

Fish, Stanley. *Is There a Text in This Class? The Authority of Interpretive Communities.* Cambridge: Harvard UP, 1980.

Forster, E. M. *Aspects of the Novel.* 1927. London: Arnold, 1974.

Franklin, H. Bruce. *The Wake of the Gods: Melville's Mythology.* Stanford: Stanford UP, 1963.

Frye, Northrop. *Anatomy of Criticism: Four Essays.* Princeton: Princeton UP, 1957.

———. *The Return of Eden: Five Essays on Milton's Epics.* Toronto: U of Toronto P, 1965.

————. *The Secular Scripture: A Study of the Structure of Romance.* Cambridge: Harvard UP, 1976.

Gilman, William H. *Melville's Early Life and* Redburn. New York: New York UP, 1951.

Gilmore, Michael T., ed. *Twentieth Century Interpretations of* Moby-Dick: *A Collection of Critical Essays.* Englewood Cliffs: Prentice, 1977.

Gleim, William S. *The Meaning of* Moby-Dick. 1938. New York: Russell, 1962.

Gottesman, Ronald, et al., eds. *The Norton Anthology of American Literature.* 2 vols. New York: Norton, 1978. Vol. 1.

Greenberg, Robert M. "Cetology: Center of Multiplicity and Discord in *Moby-Dick.*" *ESQ* 27 (1981): 1–13.

Gross, Theodore L., and Stanley Wertheim. *Hawthorne, Melville, Stephen Crane: A Critical Bibliography.* New York: Free, 1971.

Grossinger, Richard. "Melville's *Whale*: A Brief Guide to the Text." *An Olson-Melville Sourcebook.* Vol. 1: *The New Found Land, North America.* Ed. Richard Grossinger. Plainfield: North Atlantic, 1976. 97–152.

Guetti, James. *The Limits of Metaphor: A Study of Melville, Conrad, and Faulkner.* Ithaca: Cornell UP, 1967.

Gullón, Ricardo. "On Space in the Novel." *Critical Inquiry* 2 (1975): 11–28.

Hawthorne, Nathaniel. *The English Notebooks.* Ed. Randall Stewart. New York: MLA, 1941.

————. *The Scarlet Letter.* Vol. 1 of *The Centenary Edition of the Works of Nathaniel Hawthorne.* Ed. William Charvat et al. Columbus: Ohio State UP, 1962.

Hayford, Harrison. "'Loomings': Yarns and Figures in the Fabric." *Artful Thunder: Versions of the Romantic Tradition in American Literature in Honor of Howard P. Vincent.* Ed. Robert J. DeMott and Sanford E. Marovitz. Kent: Kent State UP, 1975. 119–37.

————. "Unnecessary Duplicates: A Key to the Writing of *Moby-Dick.*" *New Perspectives on Melville.* Ed. Faith Pullin. Kent: Kent State UP, 1978. 128–61.

Hayford, Harrison, and Hershel Parker, eds. *Moby-Dick.* By Herman Melville. New York: Norton, 1967. All quotations from—and page references to—*Moby-Dick* refer to this edition.

Heffernan, Thomas Farel. *Stove by a Whale: Owen Chase and the* Essex. Middletown: Wesleyan UP, 1981.

Herbert, T. Walter, Jr. Moby-Dick *and Calvinism: A World Dismantled.* New Brunswick: Rutgers UP, 1977.

Higgins, Brian. *Herman Melville: An Annotated Bibliography.* Vol. 1: *1846–1930.* Boston: Hall, 1979.

Hillway, Tyrus, and Luther S. Mansfield, eds. Moby-Dick *Centennial Essays.* Dallas: Southern Methodist UP, 1953.

Hoffman, Daniel G. *Form and Fable in American Fiction.* New York: Oxford UP, 1961.

Holland, Norman N. *The Dynamics of Literary Response.* 1968. New York: Norton, 1975.

Horkheimer, Max, and Theodor Adorno. *Dialectic of Enlightenment*. Trans. J. Cumming. New York: Herder, 1972.

Horsford, Howard C. "The Design of the Argument in *Moby-Dick*." *Modern Fiction Studies* 8 (1962): 233–51.

Howard, Leon. *Herman Melville*. U of Minnesota Pamphlets on American Writers 13. Minneapolis: U of Minnesota P, 1961.

———. *Herman Melville: A Biography*. Berkeley: U of California P, 1951.

Hunsberger, Claude. "Vectors in Recent *Moby-Dick* Criticism." *College Literature* 2 (1975): 230–45.

Irey, Eugene F. *A Concordance to Herman Melville's* Moby-Dick. 2 vols. New York: Garland, 1982.

Irwin, John T. *American Hieroglyphics: The Symbol of the Egyptian Hieroglyphics in the American Renaissance*. New Haven: Yale UP, 1980.

Kant, Immanuel. *Critique of Pure Reason*. Trans. Norman Kemp Smith. New York: St. Martin's, 1961.

Karcher, Carolyn L. *Shadow over the Promised Land: Slavery, Race and Violence in Melville's America*. Baton Rouge: Louisiana State UP, 1980.

Kawin, Bruce F. *The Mind of the Novel: Reflexive Fiction and the Ineffable*. Princeton: Princeton UP, 1982.

Kern, Edith. *The Absolute Comic*. New York: Columbia UP, 1980.

Kuhn, Thomas. *The Structure of Scientific Revolutions*. Chicago: U of Chicago P, 1962.

Kulkarni, H. B. Moby-Dick: *A Hindu Avatar—A Study of Myth and Thought in* Moby-Dick. Logan: Utah State U Monograph Series, 1970.

Lawrence, D. H. *Studies in Classic American Literature*. 1923. New York: Anchor-Doubleday, 1953.

Lentricchia, Frank. *After the New Criticism*. Chicago: U of Chicago P, 1980.

Lesser, Simon O. *Fiction and the Unconscious*. Boston: Beacon, 1957.

Leverenz, David. "*Moby-Dick*." *Psychoanalysis and Literary Process*. Ed. Frederick Crews. Cambridge: Winthrop, 1970. 66–117.

Levin, Harry. *The Power of Blackness: Poe, Hawthorne, Melville*. New York: Knopf, 1958.

Levin, David, and Theodore L. Gross, eds. *America in Literature*. 2 vols. New York: Wiley, 1978. Vol. 1.

Lewis, R. W. B. *The American Adam: Innocence, Tragedy, and Tradition in the Nineteenth Century*. Chicago: U of Chicago P, 1955.

Leyda, Jay. *The Melville Log: A Documentary Life of Herman Melville*. 2 vols. 1951. Rpt. with supplement, New York: Gordian, 1969.

MacCaffrey, Isabel. *Spenser's Allegory: The Anatomy of Imagination*. Princeton: Princeton UP, 1976.

MacShane, Frank. "Conrad on Melville." *American Literature* 29 (1958): 463–64.

Macy, Obed. *History of Nantucket*. Boston: Hillard, 1935.

Mandel, Barrett J. "What's at the Bottom of Literature?" *College English* 38 (1976): 250–60.

Mansfield, Luther S., and Howard P. Vincent, eds. *Moby-Dick; or, The Whale.* New York: Hendricks, 1952.

Martin, Terence. *Teaching a Novel:* Moby-Dick *in the Classroom.* New York: College Entrance Examination Board, 1965.

Marx, Leo. *The Machine in the Garden: Technology and the Pastoral Ideal in America.* New York: Oxford UP, 1964.

Mason, Ronald. *The Spirit above the Dust.* 2nd ed. Mamaroneck: Appel, 1972.

Mather, Cotton. *Magnalia Christi Americana.* 1702. 2 vols. Hartford, 1820.

Matthiessen, F. O. *American Renaissance: Art and Expression in the Age of Emerson and Whitman.* New York: Oxford UP, 1941.

McCarthy, Paul. "A Note on Teaching *Moby-Dick.*" *ESQ* 35 (1964): 73–79.

Melville, Herman. *Moby-Dick; or, The Whale.* Illus. Barry Moser. 1979. Berkeley: U of California P, 1981.

Melville Society Extracts. Melville Soc. of America, 1969–

Metcalf, Eleanor Melville. *Herman Melville: Cycle and Epicycle.* Cambridge: Harvard UP, 1953.

Milder, Robert. "The Composition of *Moby-Dick*: A Review and a Prospect." *ESQ* 23 (1977): 203–16.

———. "'Knowing' Melville." *ESQ* 24 (1978): 96–117.

Miller, Edwin H. *Melville.* New York: Braziller, 1975.

Miller, James E., Jr. *A Reader's Guide to Herman Melville.* New York: Noonday-Farrar, 1962.

Miller, Perry. *The Raven and the Whale: The War of Words and Wits in the Era of Poe and Melville.* New York: Harcourt, 1956.

Minter, David L. *The Interpreted Design as a Structural Principle in American Prose.* New Haven: Yale UP, 1969.

Murray, Henry A. "Definitions of Myth." *The Making of Myth.* Ed. Richard M. Ohmann. New York: Putnam, 1962. 7–37.

———. "In nomine diaboli." *New England Quarterly* 24 (1951): 435–52. Rpt. in Chase, *Melville* 62–74.

Mushabac, Jane. *Melville's Humor.* Hamden: Archon, 1981.

Nechas, James William. *Synonomy, Repetition, and Restatement in the Vocabulary of Herman Melville's* Moby-Dick. Norwood: Norwood, 1978.

Olson, Charles. *Call Me Ishmael.* 1947. New York: Grove, 1958.

Ong, Walter J. *Interfaces of the Word.* Ithaca: Cornell UP, 1977.

Otto, Rudolf. *The Idea of the Holy.* Trans. John W. Harvey. Rev. ed. London: Oxford UP, 1928.

Oxford Annotated Bible with the Apocrypha: Revised Standard Version. Ed. Herbert G. May and Bruce M. Metzger. New York: Oxford UP, 1965.

Parker, Hershel. "Five Reviews Not in Moby-Dick *as Doubloon.*" *English Language Notes* 9 (1972): 182–85.

———. "Herman Melville." Gottesman et al. 2032–44.

———. "Practical Editions: *Moby-Dick.*" *Proof* 3 (1973): 371–78.

———, ed. *The Recognition of Herman Melville.* Ann Arbor: U of Michigan P, 1967.

Parker, Hershel, and Harrison Hayford, eds. Moby-Dick *as Doubloon: Essays and Extracts (1851–1970).* New York: Norton, 1970.

Percival, M. O. *A Reading of* Moby-Dick. Chicago: U of Chicago P, 1950.

Pommer, Henry F. *Milton and Melville.* Pittsburgh: U of Pittsburgh P, 1950.

Reed, Walter L. *Meditations on the Hero: A Study of the Romantic Hero in Nine-teenth-Century Fiction.* New Haven: Yale UP, 1974.

Reno, Janet. "Ishmael Alone Escaped: *Moby-Dick* as a Survivor's Narrative." Diss. George Washington Univ., 1983.

Richards, I. A. *Practical Criticism.* 1929. New York: Harcourt, 1963.

Ricks, Beatrice, and Joseph Adams. *Herman Melville: A Reference Bibliography.* Boston: Hall, 1973.

Rogin, Michael Paul. *Subversive Genealogy: The Politics and Art of Herman Melville.* New York: Knopf, 1983.

Roper, Gordon. "On Teaching *Moby-Dick.*" *ESQ* 29 (1962): 2–4.

Rosenberry, Edward H. *Melville and the Comic Spirit.* Cambridge: Harvard UP, 1955.

Sachs, Viola. "The Gnosis of Hawthorne and Melville: An Interpretation of *The Scarlet Letter* and *Moby-Dick.*" *American Quarterly* 32 (1980): 123–40.

Scheick, William J. Introduction. *The Life and Death of That Reverend Man of God, Mr. Richard Mather.* Bainbridge: York Mail-Print, 1974.

Sealts, Merton M., Jr. "Approaching Melville through 'Hawthorne and His Mosses.'" *ESQ* 28 (1962): 12–15.

———. *The Early Lives of Melville: Nineteenth Century Biographical Sketches and Their Authors.* Madison: U of Wisconsin P, 1974.

———, ed. *The Journals and Miscellaneous Notebooks of Ralph Waldo Emerson.* Vol. 5: 1835–38. Cambridge: Harvard UP, 1965.

———. *Melville's Reading: A Check-List of Books Owned and Borrowed.* Madison: U of Wisconsin P, 1966.

———. *Pursuing Melville: 1940–1980.* Madison: U of Wisconsin P, 1982.

Sedgwick, William Ellery. *Herman Melville: The Tragedy of Mind.* Cambridge: Harvard UP, 1944.

Seelye, John. *Melville: The Ironic Diagram.* Evanston: Northwestern UP, 1970.

Sewall, Richard. *The Vision of Tragedy.* New Haven: Yale UP, 1959.

Sherrill, Rowland A. *The Prophetic Melville: Experience, Transcendence, and Trag-edy.* Athens: U of Georgia P, 1979.

Shurr, William H. *Rappaccini's Children: American Writers in a Calvinistic World.* Lexington: UP of Kentucky, 1981.

Simpson, David. *Fetishism and Imagination: Dickens, Melville, Conrad.* Baltimore: Johns Hopkins UP, 1982.

Slotkin, Richard. *Regeneration through Violence: The Mythology of the American Frontier, 1600–1860.* Middletown: Wesleyan UP, 1973.

Stanzel, Franz. *Narrative Situations in the Novel.* Trans. James P. Pusack. Bloomington: Indiana UP, 1971.

Stern, Milton R., ed. *Discussions of* Moby-Dick. Boston: Heath, 1960.

———. *The Fine Hammered Steel of Herman Melville.* Urbana: U of Illinois P, 1957.

———. "The Whale and the Minnow: *Moby-Dick* and the Movies." *College English* 17 (1956): 470–73.

Stewart, George R. "The Two *Moby-Dicks.*" *American Literature* 25 (1954): 417–48.

Sweeney, Gerard M. *Melville's Use of Classical Mythology.* Amsterdam: Rodopi, 1975.

Tanselle, G. Thomas. *A Checklist of Editions of* Moby-Dick, *1851–1976.* Chicago: Northwestern UP and the Newberry Library, 1976.

Thompson, Lawrance. *Melville's Quarrel with God.* Princeton: Princeton UP, 1952.

Thoreau, Henry David. *Walden.* 1854. Ed. J. Lyndon Shanley. Princeton: Princeton UP, 1971.

Ujházy, Maria. *Herman Melville's World of Whaling.* Hungary: Akadémiai Kiadó, 1983.

Updike, John. "Melville's Withdrawal." *Hugging the Shore: Essays and Criticism.* New York: Knopf, 1983. 80–106.

Vann, J. Don. "A Selected Checklist of Melville Criticism, 1958–68." *Studies in the Novel* 4 (1969): 507–35.

VanSickle, Dirck. *Montana Gothic.* New York: Harcourt, 1979.

Vargish, Thomas. "Gnostic *Mythos* in *Moby-Dick.*" *PMLA* 81 (1966): 272–77.

Vincent, Howard P., ed. *Charles E. Merrill Studies in* Moby-Dick. Columbus: Merrill, 1969.

———. "Ishmael, Writer and Art Critic." *Themes and Directions in American Literature: Essays in Honor of Leon Howard.* Ed. Ray B. Browne and Donald Pizer. Lafayette: Purdue UP, 1969. 69–79.

———. *The Trying-Out of* Moby-Dick. 1949. Kent: Kent State UP, 1980.

Wadlington, Warwick. "Ishmael's Godly Gamesomeness: Selftaste and Rhetoric in *Moby-Dick.*" *The Confidence Game in American Literature.* Princeton: Princeton UP, 1975. 73–103.

Ward, Joseph A. "The Function of the Cetological Chapters in *Moby-Dick.*" *American Literature* 28 (1956): 168–83.

Warren, Robert Penn, ed. *Selected Poems of Herman Melville.* New York: Random, 1967.

Werge, Thomas. "*Moby-Dick* and the Calvinist Tradition." *Studies in the Novel* 1 (1969): 484–506.

Wertmüller, Lina. *The Head of Alvise*. New York: Morrow, 1982.

Whitman, Walt. *Leaves of Grass: Comprehensive Reader's Edition*. Ed. Harold W. Blodgett and Sculley Bradley. New York: Norton, 1968.

Woodress, James, ed. *Eight American Authors*. Rev. ed. New York: Norton, 1971.

Wright, Nathalia. "Herman Melville." Woodress 173–224.

———. *Melville's Use of the Bible*. Durham: Duke UP, 1949.

Young, James Dean. "The Nine Gams of the *Pequod*." *American Literature* 25 (1954): 449–63.

Zoellner, Robert. *The Salt-Sea Mastodon: A Reading of* Moby-Dick. Berkeley: U of California P, 1973.

Films

Herman Melville: November in My Soul. CBS-TV, 1978.

Huston, John, dir. *Moby-Dick*. Warner Brothers, 1956.

Mudge, Jean McClure, writer. Richard Wilbur, narr. *Herman Melville: Consider the Sea*. International Film Bureau, 1982. (Information available from International Film Bureau, 332 S. Michigan Ave., Chicago, IL 60604.)

A Whaling Voyage. Educational Development Center. Condensation of *Down to the Sea in Ships*, 1922 silent feature. (Information available from Educational Development Center, 55 Chapel St., Newton, MA 02160.)

INDEX